DISCIPLE MAKING

Disciple Making

Raising Another Up Toward Maturity in Christ

REVISED EDITION

John R. Kimball

with
Gayle Buford

BEAUMEADOW
GROUP

Disciple Making
REVISED EDITION

Copyright© 2019, 2023 John Kimball

ISBN: 979-8-9858423-2-6

All rights reserved.

No part of this book may be used or reproduced stored in a retrieval system, or transmitted in any form or by any means—electronic, mechanical, photocopy, recording, or any other manner—without the prior written permission from the author, except in case of brief quotations embodied in critical articles and reviews.

Scripture quotations taken from the THE HOLY BIBLE, NEW INTERNATIONAL VERSION®, NIV® Copyright © 1973, 1978, 1984, 2011 by Biblica, Inc.® Used by permission. All rights reserved worldwide.

Cover design, Layout and Format: Kim Gardell, Graphic Design

Published in the United States of America by
The Beaumeadow Group
Oviedo, Florida

www.beaumeadow.com

ACKNOWLEDGEMENTS

Even in a simple book like this one, there are so many people that I must thank. First and foremost, my gratitude goes to Gayle Buford for her hours of work listening to the sermon series that planted the seeds for this text, and for pouring over my various notes and writings on the subject to compile a truly readable result. While I may be the author, Gayle is truly the writer of what you now have in front of you.

Second, I must express my ongoing thanks to the leadership team of Palmwood Church of Oviedo, Florida — Bob Buford, Stephen O'Guin and Danny Eshcol — for co-laboring with me in the gospel ministry. They are gospel-hearted, harvest-focused folks that help keep me on the right track, bearing fruit for Jesus. I am grateful.

Third, I would like to thank Chrissy Hoffman and the excellent staff of the Oviedo YMCA for the incredible, daily ministry partnership we enjoy together keeping Christ central in the story and function of the Oviedo Family Center. And thanks also to Archie Adams, Director of Christian Initiatives and Lead Chaplain for the YMCA of Central Florida, for the ongoing opportunity to serve the precious membership of the Oviedo Family Center as their Chaplain.

Fourth, I would be remiss if I did not thank my friends and mentors, Tom Johnston and Mike Chong Perkinson of the Praxis Center for Church Development. Tom and Mike have literally invested in me and my ministry efforts for the last fifteen years — and without them, their wisdom, their guidance and their resourcing, I would still be a pastor making many of the mistakes I address in this book. The personal foundation of everything in this book began with their tutelage and some of the material is directly from their own ministries. And so I enthusiastically commend to you the training and resources of the Praxis Center *(www.praxiscenter.org)*. You and your church will be blessed.

Finally, I must thank my ministry partner and encourager of nearly 35 years, my bride Kathryn. She's urged me on, encouraged me to seek training and wise counsel, and she's (frankly) kept me from quitting when the going got really tough. I love you.

It is my prayer that this book blesses you, your ministry and the kingdom of our God. Thank you for reading it.

PREFACE

Then Jesus came to them and said, "All authority in heaven and on earth has been given to me. Therefore go and make disciples of all nations, baptizing them in the name of the Father and of the Son and of the Holy Spirit, and teaching them to obey everything I have commanded you. And surely I am with you always, to the very end of the age." (Matthew 28:18-20 NIV)

The Great Commission: Jesus' last instructions to his disciples as recorded by Matthew.

Most Christians believe it is important to obey Jesus. Christians and their respective churches do many things in pursuit of obedience — preaching, outreach, youth and children's ministry, Bible studies and more — but most are not effectively doing the one thing Jesus commissioned us all to do: make disciples. We want to do what he asks, yet I am not sure the church at large today has equipped us adequately for this particular assignment. The church (particularly in North America) has concentrated on telling and teaching others about Jesus, but has perhaps misunderstood or focused only in part on what it means to *"go and make disciples of all nations."* We seem to substitute telling others about Jesus in place of making disciples for Jesus. The commandment was not to simply to tell people about Jesus, to make believers, or even to make good church members. It was to *go* and make *disciples.* What's the difference between a believer and a disciple? Is our job finished when we lead someone to faith in Christ and invite them to church to hear good teaching? If not, why not?

Disciple making is a process, not an event. Disciple making is a commandment given by the one who has *"all authority in heaven and on earth."* If we are to fulfill The Great Commission, we must obey everything He has commanded. In order to obey, we must understand. This book is intended to help believers do that.

We will begin by defining what a disciple is. Ever try to put together a jigsaw puzzle without looking at the picture on the box? Ever try to assemble a kit from IKEA full of wooden or plastic pieces, metal rods, and screws of various sizes without an instruction manual and its pictures? Frustrating at best; impossible at worst. Making disciples without a model to follow would be the same. Fortunately, Jesus did not leave us clueless. He gave us both a model and all the necessary instructions.

Once we understand what we are expected to do, we can begin the process of partnering with the Creator of the Universe in the making of disciples. In the chapters that follow, we will get the instructions we need to create those disciples for Jesus. More accurately, we can join with God himself in the creation of disciples. We will come to realize that "disciple" is both a noun and a verb. We are commanded to go and make disciples. In order to do so, we must disciple those disciples — *teaching them to obey everything [Jesus has] commanded.* In fact, the real goal is to make disciples that make disciples! We will learn that disciple making is far more than bringing our new converts to church so that they can go through a class or listen to some good, biblical preaching.

With whom should we do the work of disciple making? Here's a hint: it's not just the new convert. We must be about this work all around us — every day. It is an effort that we do in partnership with Jesus' Church. *Go and make disciples of all nations.*

Sounds daunting? Fear not! We not only have God's instructions in this process, we have our very own helper and guide in the person of the Holy Spirit. Remember, the commandment ends with, *"surely I am with you always, to the very end of the age."*

TABLE OF CONTENTS

ACKNOWLEDGEMENTS v

PREFACE vii

CHAPTER ONE 1
   Make Disciples of All Nations

CHAPTER TWO 19
   A Disciple is Devoted to Jesus

CHAPTER THREE 35
   A Disciple is Devoted to Jesus' People, the Church

CHAPTER FOUR 55
   A Disciple is Devoted to Jesus' Mission– His Passion

CHAPTER FIVE 75
   Disciples Make Disciples

CHAPTER SIX 89
   Disciples Are "All In"

CHAPTER ONE
Make Disciples of All Nations

Then Jesus came to them and said, "All authority in heaven and on earth has been given to me. Therefore go and make disciples of all nations, baptizing them in the name of the Father and of the Son and of the Holy Spirit, and teaching them to obey everything I have commanded you. And surely I am with you always, to the very end of the age." (Matthew 28:18-20 NIV)

Christians and their respective churches do many good things — preaching, outreach, youth and children's ministry, bible studies, and much more. But most are not very effective in doing the one thing Jesus commissioned us to do. In fact, some of the unchurched around us may understand The Great Commission better than many church folks. Many of the unchurched understand that they need help. They understand that they lack a meaningful connection with God; but unfortunately, they often don't see the help they need coming from the church. Sadly, according to church researcher Thom Arn, about 80% of churches in the United States are either in plateau or decline.[1] How heartbreaking! This indicates that God's kingdom is not growing and expanding. If we were fulfilling The Great Commission as we should, this could not happen.

In my role as a ministry coach and mentor, I work with churches in decline. I see the same patterns again and again. These churches are doing many things right. They typically teach sound doctrine. They focus on service and see the need for outreach. They invest a great deal of time and energy in providing meaningful worship experiences for their congregants each week. What is missing is that they have stopped investing in the next spiritual generation, drawing them close to the heart of Jesus. They have stopped making disciples.

Somewhere around the 1950s or 60s, it seems that Sunday School became a largely academic exercise. Students were provided the opportunity to learn about Jesus, but rarely were they provided transformational disciple making experiences that actually help them become more like Jesus. Information is not necessarily transformation. The teacher prepares each week and delivers excellent material, but rarely is the expectation and accountability laid on the student for an application that results in a changed life.

I once heard a story that may indeed be true, of an older, wise retired pastor who was serving as an interim preacher for a congregation in transition between regular pastors. On his first Sunday, he preached what everyone agreed was an exceptionally

---

[1] The State of the American Church, malphursgroup.com, 2018.

wonderful sermon. The deacons, and everyone else in the congregation for that matter, were ecstatic with anticipation for what messages were to come throughout his term of service. When the next week arrived, the interim preacher preached the very same sermon! Few questioned this choice. After all, the message was exceptional and there had been many who were absent that first Sunday. They all needed to hear that message. The next week came. Same sermon. After week four, when the sermon was again exactly the same, the deacons called a meeting with the interim preacher to question why he continued to just repeat the same sermon week after week. Were they to expect this lack of creativity for the whole term of his service? He responded, "I'm so glad that you've recognized this as the same sermon each week! Now, when you begin to implement that lesson, we'll move on to the next one!" When it comes to learning from the Word of God, we need to be doers, not just hearers. We need to be appliers, not just admirers.

Curricula explaining who Jesus is and what he has done abound, but tools of transformation into Christ-likeness are far too scarce. Our task is not to memorize and recite The Great Commission or to cross stitch it into artwork to adorn the walls of our churches, but rather it is to understand what it truly means to apply this challenge to go and make disciples who obey everything Jesus commands.

How can we do this? We must understand what it is Jesus is commanding us to do. We must learn what it looks like to make disciples, and then we must apply what we have learned.

DISCIPLE MAKING

Many Christians approach the Great Commission with a measure of fear and trepidation. In part, this fear is because they do not understand what this call to disciple making is really asking of them. Visions of gospel confrontations, long explanations of bible passages and having to defend doctrine or other aspects of the faith make folks shake in their boots. Fortunately, this is not Jesus' way. He models the process for us in the gospels. In this book, we will examine the model closely, starting at the beginning.

When does disciple making begin? Most church-goers, and even most pastors, would probably answer that the process begins as soon as someone accepts Christ as Savior. But that's not exactly correct. Disciple making actually begins before a person surrenders to Jesus. It's a journey that must include evangelism, but it does not always begin with evangelism. We disciple people toward conversion. We disciple people through conversion. And we disciple people from conversion toward maturity in Christ. Disciple making is the whole spectrum.

When did Jesus, our example, start making disciples of his twelve? He started when they began to follow him. And none of them were believers at that point! So, like Jesus, we must start with people who don't yet know and understand Jesus. Disciple making begins there and continues until a person is led into fruit-bearing maturity — they become disciples who make disciples. *That* is the task to which we are called by The Great Commission.

Let's discuss to whom this commission is addressed. It is clearly addressed to the church — the body of believers who have committed themselves to further the kingdom rule and reign of Christ. The Great Commission gives the church direction and purpose. Many Christians, including many pastors, believe that the purpose of the church is worship. Rather, that is the purpose of humanity. Isaiah 43:7 tells us that God made us for his glory. The very first question and subsequent answer of the Westminster Catechism, familiar to a great many children of the Reformed tradition, so states: "*Q. What is the chief end of man? A. Man's chief end is to glorify God, and to enjoy him forever.*" Humanity's purpose is worship. The purpose given to the Church by our Lord is to make disciples — to make worshipers.

We are commanded to make disciples *of all nations*. The Greek word translated here as *nations* is *ethne*, from which we get the English words *ethnic* and *ethnicity*. *Ethne* refers to a people group who share a common language and set of customs, in short, a culture. In Acts 1:8, Jesus tells his disciples just before he leaves them to be taken up into heaven: *"But you will receive power when the Holy Spirit comes on you; and you will be my witnesses in Jerusalem, and in all Judea and Samaria, and to the ends of the earth."* (Acts 1:8 NIV) Jerusalem, Judea, Samaria, and the ends of the earth. Like those early Christians, we follow a similar plan.

These four arenas of mission were concentric circles for those early Jewish Christians. *Jerusalem* represented home; the culture most familiar to them. *Judea* represented a larger geographic area, but where the culture was largely still familiar. *Samaria* was like Judea's culture in many ways but was still the first step cross-culturally. The *ends of the earth* were peoples whose lands and cultures were radically different from their own.

In modern terms, we might think of our Jerusalem as our own neighborhood, community, or circle of associates. Our Judea might represent the larger surrounding area with which we are familiar, perhaps our town, county or region where the culture is still much like ours. Samaria could include an even wider geographical area, perhaps including new language groups. When the disciples thought of Samaria, they would have thought of a similar but different culture whose customs and language was somewhat familiar. Today, many of us live near folks who speak a different native language and have different customs. This would be our Samaria. Finally, *the ends of the earth* — places far from us whose language and culture are totally foreign. This is what we think of as foreign missions: places we have endeavored to send missionaries. Yet for many of us today, Samaria, and even the "ends of the earth" have actually come to us. In the Orlando metropolitan area in which I live, we are surrounded by people from all over the world. These people have come to our region to live and to work, dressing differently, speaking different languages, and having different priorities and values. For many of us reading this book, we don't even have to leave our communities to find our "Jerusalem, Judea, Samaria, and the ends of the earth." These all are our potential disciples, even though they may presently know nothing, or almost nothing, of Christ.

We are commanded to *go and make disciples*. A more accurate understanding of the word "go" here comes from its Greek grammar. It's not a single word or imperative but actually a participial phrase. You might think of our "ing" words in English. A better translation might be, "going," "as you go" or "as you are going." Jesus told his disciples, "As you are going, make disciples." Arguably, this is less of a command to go and more of an expectation that we are already doing that. Jesus knew that those to whom he was speaking would be going about their daily lives, as will we. It's as if Jesus was saying, "People, you're going to be going through life anyway, so as you are going, make disciples along the way." As we are going, we should think of our disciple making task not as the response to a command, but as part of our DNA. Every day, everywhere we go, in every relationship we have, we are to be making disciples.

What if disciple making is not about arguments and challenging people's philosophies? Oh those things might happen *as we are going*, but it will be in the context of relationship and will usually happen in friendly conversation. Disciple making is not simply about dragging people across the threshold of belief in Christ, but more about living life together so that the Spirit can use us to gently nudge people, slowly and surely, closer to Jesus and then on to maturity in their faith. Jesus isn't calling us to be argumentative. We don't need to be "experts" to make disciples. We're actually supposed to make disciples among family, friends, coworkers and others all the time. Of course some might require a concerted effort, but most will be influenced slowly "as we go"…together.

As those relationships with the people we encounter as we go deepen and as the disciple making process progresses, there are imperatives in The Great Commission. One of the most important is baptism — *baptizing them in the name of the Father and of the Son and of the Holy Spirit.*

In the United States where I live, baptism is often thought of as a sweet symbolic gesture. It certainly is symbolic of washing away our sin and the cleansing of our nature. It symbolizes our death (going down into the water), burial (under the water) and resurrection (coming up out of the water) with Christ, but there's more.

Baptism carries a profound meaning for many of our Christian brothers and sisters in other lands; especially in lands where it is challenging or even dangerous to follow Jesus. In the first century baptism was costly. It was considered treasonous in the early Roman empire. In the first century, baptism and its declaration of Jesus' lordship flew directly in the face of Caesar's lordship. People died over this! Believers in places like North Korea, Somalia, Yemen and Afghanistan still experience that danger today. In other lands dominated by other religions, baptism and its declaration of Jesus' lordship is a public replacement of their gods — gods that the rest of the baptism candidate's family may still follow. It is still true that a full allegiance to Jesus divides families (see Matthew 10:32-39).

You see, baptism is a declaration of radical allegiance to our King. That is our King with a capital "K." We are baptized into the name of our King. When we are baptized, we are joining ourselves in a covenant relationship with the Lord of our lives. In baptism, we are publicly declaring, "I am a Jesus-follower. He is now and forever my everything."

Baptism is a line of demarcation. It says, "I belong to Jesus alone." It is a public declaration of a singular covenant relationship, much like marriage. It boldly and publicly proclaims, "I am now taking the name of Jesus." When Jesus commissions us to "[baptize] them in the *name* of the Father and of the Son and of the Holy Spirit," it is a clear call to separate those new disciples unto our Triune God for his purposes. Paul refers to these commissioned workers as Christ's ambassadors (2 Corinthians 5:20). Baptism is a great and wonderful thing to celebrate — but make no mistake, it is also a declaration of pre-eminent allegiance to the King of all kings. That declaration can be costly.

A story from my own life illustrates this quite well. During one of my two trips to Japan, a young woman was assigned to me as a translator for my sermons and conversations. She served me quite well. Near the end of my trip, I realized I knew little about her as a person, so over lunch one day I asked her to tell me her story. With tear-rimmed eyes, she told me that she was childless and that her unbelieving husband blamed her barrenness on her having become a Christian. Years before, she had connecting with a Christian missionary family. Through their loving witness, she started attending their church and eventually surrendered to Jesus. She openly shared this with her family. It was fine with them as long as Jesus was just a curiosity — one of the "gods on the shelf." In fact, it remained that way for years until the day she told them that she had been baptized. On that day, her father declared her dead and held her funeral. Her family's Shinto religion regarded all their dead ancestors as protectors and guides for the living. By declaring her exclusive faith in Jesus, he told everyone that she had broken her ties with her family and her heritage. She was never welcome again.

The second imperative following Jesus' expectation to make disciples as we go is about teaching. Many think Jesus said to "teach them everything I have commanded you." But that is incorrect. He said to "teach them TO OBEY everything I have commanded you." Knowledge and obedience are two different things entirely. While we must have knowledge in order to obey, teaching knowledge alone is disobedience. To teach obedience, we must demonstrate obedience to Christ's commands ourselves. The concept of teaching here is not simply academic — not about passing on information. It's about fostering transformation. We must be partners with Jesus in transforming a life. It cannot be taught by lecture. It must be instilled life-on-life, just as Jesus did with his disciples. This kind of teaching is the heart of disciple making.

A disciple is a student, but not just one who learns facts and knowledge. Rather, he or she is one who learns to apply facts and knowledge in order to obediently honor God by expanding his kingdom rule and reign. A disciple's understanding is not primarily demonstrated in what they know and say, but in how they live! Mentoring is the way this is be accomplished. For this reason, our church has chosen as our mission statement: Loving God Extravagantly — Loving People with Humility — Mentoring Others to do the Same. It is the last part of the statement, the "mentoring others to do the same" by which the imperative *teaching them to obey everything I have commanded you* is fulfilled.

We must realize that disciple making is a process, not a singular event. Because the church in the West tends to focus on evangelism where "success" is defined as leading someone to say "yes" to Jesus, well-meaning Christians often feel they have failed when spiritual conversations do not lead to a decision for Christ. Conversion to Christ is not our job! It is the Holy Spirit's work to convict of sin and to do the work of conversion. We are simply tools in the process. Jesus makes this clear in John 16:5-11.

One of the most transformative experiences of my life took place in 1995 when my wife and I visited The Cove, Billy Graham's retreat center in North Carolina. While there we got to meet some of the greats of the faith: George Beverly Shea, Franklin Graham and others, but the most impactful to me was a man named Jim Engel. Jim Engel published a book, now out of print, *What's Wrong with the Harvest?*[2] In that book he included a tool called The Engel Scale of Evangelism (see next page). Examine it carefully. Where is the point of conversion? It is only half way through the process!

As we discussed earlier, Western Christians tend to think of success in disciple making in terms of leading someone to make a decision for Christ. The Engel Scale shows us that what we've been calling success is only one point on a larger scale. Disciple making is not just the number of conversions we see — how many times we led people in the sinner's prayer — there's much more.

Let's take the example of a conversation you have with your neighbor who only has a vague awareness of the supernatural and no effective knowledge of Christianity at all. If at the end of your conversation, or multiple conversations over a period of time, that neighbor has an awareness of what Christianity really is, you've done successful disciple making. You've partnered with the Holy Spirit to move them one step closer to new birth in Christ! Don't believe the lie that, because they did not ask Christ into their life in that moment, you've failed. This is how Satan sows seeds of defeat to keep us from continuing to make disciples.

If you've engaged someone who has moved even one step along the scale, you've been an effective witness for Christ. Bill Bright and other leaders have said that the average North American needs to have a relevant confrontation with the gospel of Jesus

---

2   *What's Wrong with the Harvest?* Zondervan, 1975.

Engle Scale of Evangelism

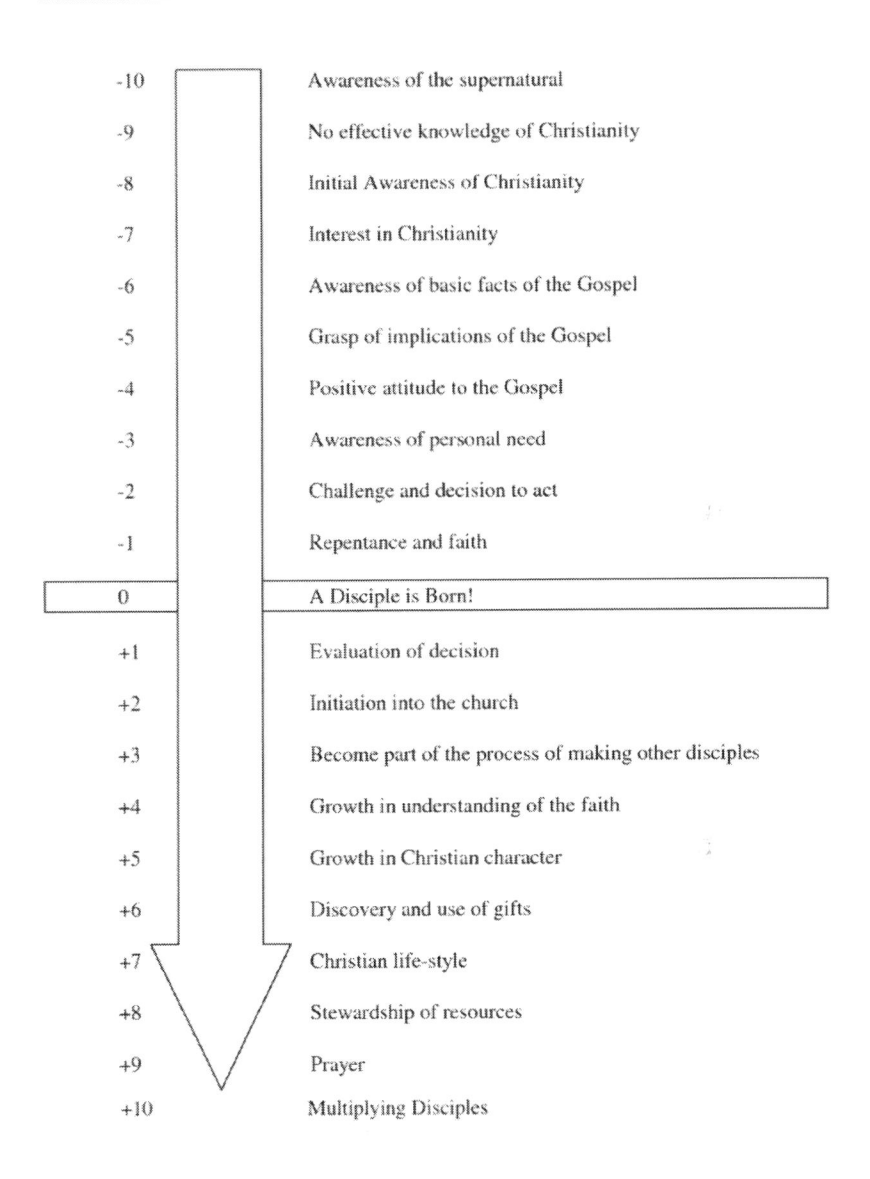

-10	Awareness of the supernatural
-9	No effective knowledge of Christianity
-8	Initial Awareness of Christianity
-7	Interest in Christianity
-6	Awareness of basic facts of the Gospel
-5	Grasp of implications of the Gospel
-4	Positive attitude to the Gospel
-3	Awareness of personal need
-2	Challenge and decision to act
-1	Repentance and faith
0	**A Disciple is Born!**
+1	Evaluation of decision
+2	Initiation into the church
+3	Become part of the process of making other disciples
+4	Growth in understanding of the faith
+5	Growth in Christian character
+6	Discovery and use of gifts
+7	Christian life-style
+8	Stewardship of resources
+9	Prayer
+10	Multiplying Disciples

Christ seven times before they make a decision to follow Jesus. So if you are number three of the seven, have you failed? And if seven is the average, that means some will need more than seven relevant conversations before they are ready to make a decision. So for that person, you may be spiritual conversation number three of twelve (or more)! The number of spiritual conversations required to lead a particular person to Christ is up to the Holy Spirit, not us. Our goal is to move people from where they are to maturity in Christ. We want them to flourish in the spiritual disciplines and begin making disciples of others.

Remember that the Enemy does not like it when someone comes to Christ. He will inevitably plant doubts in the mind of the new believer. A new believer needs a mentor, a more mature believer, to come alongside and stand with them to reassure them that doubts are normal and that the experience is indeed real, not based on emotion, but truth. If the new believer is to become a mature disciple of Christ, they need to continue to move along that scale. Point zero, conversion, is not the goal. They will need to be taught to grow in Christlike character, to pray, and to plug into the lives of others in such a way that they begin to multiply disciples themselves. Even making sure the new believer becomes grounded in a Bible-believing, disciple making church fellowship requires a mentor. Lots of churches teach truths of the Bible, but do not make disciples.

Disciple making, then, is a journey, not a point. Sometimes we are used of the Holy Spirit on the front end of the Engel Scale; sometimes on the back end. By considering the disciple making process in terms of the scale, we clearly see that the process is far bigger than just giving someone information about becoming a Christian and praying for them to make a decision to live for Jesus. We must begin where people are and disciple them toward belief. After they reach the point of belief, we must continue to disciple them through the conversion process to maturity, always working at the direction of the Holy Spirit.

And surely I am with you always, to the very end of the age. Jesus closes out the commission of his followers in a most precious way…he promises that he will be with us always. This makes sense, because he was promised to be, and is, our *Immanuel* — "God with us." As we go through life and are open to the leading of the Spirit to nudge people toward Christ, and then on to maturity in their faith; as we baptize people, calling them to radical allegiance to King Jesus; as we mentor people toward obedience to King Jesus, extending and expanding his kingdom rule and reign, our King promises to be with us always.

Finally, on what basis does God judge our disciple making successful? The real answer to this question set me free. While it is indeed true that people often feel like they have failed when they share their faith and the person does not turn to Christ, nothing could be further from the truth. But the Father of Lies works hard to sow discouragement wherever he can. In reality, if you are able to nudge a person closer to falling in love with Jesus, or after conversion, closer toward maturity and fruit-bearing faithfulness, you have *succeeded* as a witness for Jesus! God judges the success of our disciple making on faithful obedience, not on results. The results are up to him. Only God can change a human heart. We can only be faithful to make disciples as we go. Learn the process. Be faithful and obedient. Stop worrying about the results. When we do, the incredible results will come.

Questions for Reflection and Application:

1. Consider some of the people from other cultures or religions who are going through life with you every day. How might you be used by the Holy Spirit to nudge these relationships closer to Christ— further down the Engel Scale of Evangelism?

2. What do you remember about your own baptism? How did you understand its significance as it relates to your commitment to Christ? What is the Holy Spirit saying to you today about that commitment?

3. Consider how you have been discipled. Has your experience been primarily informational, or has someone taken the time and effort to lead you in the kind of radical transformation toward Christ-likeness referred to on the Engel Scale? What steps might you need to take to seek this kind of discipling for yourself?

4. Reflect on Jesus's name, *Immanuel*. What assurance does this give you specifically as you go about the task of disciple making?

CHAPTER TWO
A Disciple is Devoted to Jesus

"The student is not above the teacher, nor a servant above his master. It is enough for students to be like their teachers, and servants like their masters. If the head of the house has been called Beelzebul, how much more the members of his household!

So do not be afraid of them, for there is nothing concealed that will not be disclosed, or hidden that will not be made known. What I tell you in the dark, speak in the daylight; what is whispered in your ear, proclaim from the roofs. Do not be afraid of those who kill the body but cannot kill the soul. Rather, be afraid of the One who can destroy both soul and body in hell. Are not two sparrows sold for a penny? Yet not one of them will fall to the ground outside your Father's care. And even the very hairs of your head are all numbered. So don't be afraid; you are worth more than many sparrows.

Whoever acknowledges me before others, I will also acknowledge before my Father in heaven. But whoever disowns me before others, I will disown before my Father in heaven.

Do not suppose that I have come to bring peace to the earth. I did not come to bring peace, but a sword. For I have come to turn a man against his father, a daughter against her mother, a daughter-in-law against her mother-in-law — a man's enemies will be the members of his own household.

Anyone who loves their father or mother more than me is not worthy of me; anyone who loves their son or daughter more than me is not worthy of me. Whoever does not take up their cross and follow me is not worthy of me. Whoever finds their life will lose it, and whoever loses their life for my sake will find it."
(Matthew 10:24-39 NIV)

If we are going to be obedient to Jesus' commission to make disciples, then we better know what a disciple looks like. In order to make a loaf of sourdough bread, we need to understand what ingredients need to go into it and how to proceed. We need a recipe. In order to make a disciple, likewise, we must understand just what a disciple is. My good friends Tom Johnston and Mike Perkinson have put together an excellent three-part definition of a disciple.[3] A disciple is devoted to Jesus, devoted

---

3   Tom Johnston and Mike Chong Perkinson, *The Organic Reformation: A New Hope for the Church in the West*, Manchester, NH: Praxis Media, 2012, pp. 70-71.

to His followers, and devoted to His mission. In this chapter, we describe the first of those three general truths about a disciple — a disciple is devoted to Jesus.

What is devotion? Understanding this word is more important than you might think. *Devotion* and *commitment* are not the same. The words are related, but the difference is crucial. Often, when people tell me they are committed Christians, I wince. People who are "committed Christians" too often mean that they are committed to the concept of Christianity. It's their religion, but they lack a vibrant love relationship with Christ. Commitment is made with the head. Devotion, on the other hand, is made in the heart. Devotion is a love response and can exist only in the context of a love relationship. Devotion is a form of love and when it comes to a relationship with Jesus it is all-encompassing. We see this in the words of Jesus, *"Jesus replied: 'Love the Lord your God with all your heart and with all your soul and with all your mind. This is the first and greatest commandment.'"* (Matthew 22:37-38 NIV) Commitment is a legal, contractual agreement. Devotion is covenantal. A contract is necessary when you deal with someone you don't trust, but a covenant is rooted in trust. Contracts may be dissolved by mutual consent of both parties. A covenant is for life. The biblical relationship with Christ is depicted as a marriage covenant. In a good, satisfying marriage, the partners are sincerely devoted to one another, not just staying together by contractual obligation. So you see, we are not looking to have someone commit to some kind of Christian agenda. Rather, we are to be about making disciples who are devoted to Jesus the Person — disciples that are head over heels in love with him and are willing to act in faithfulness and obedience.

Just as in our illustration of making bread, we need to take action. We cannot simply throw the right ingredients together in a bowl and hope it becomes bread. Likewise, there are defining actions disciples must exhibit. Devotion, like love, requires decision and action. Throughout both the Old and New Testaments, the illustration used for the devotion we are describing is marriage. From the earliest days of the Hebrew people to the era of the New Testament, God has exemplified the covenant relationship he desires to have with us in terms of marriage. Whether you're talking about Hosea redeeming a harlot (Gomer) and taking her as his wife, the imagery of the wedding banquet in Jesus' teaching, or Paul's description of how husbands and wives love each other: *"Husbands, love your wives just as Christ loved the church and gave himself up for her..."* (Ephesians 5:25 NIV), the theme is clear. Our relationship with Jesus is best exemplified by a godly marriage relationship. People in good marriages will quickly understand the joy and depth that comes with true devotion. People outside of those marriages — often people who themselves are not even married — can see the difference. We are to be that devoted to our Savior.

First, devotion **knows.** It is completely impossible to be devoted to someone you don't know. Some in the church are claiming commitment to Jesus, and that may be accurate. Commitment to Jesus is as far as the relationship goes because they do not actually know the Savior. All they can do is commit themselves to the rituals and traditions of Christianity. True devotion requires a real, personal relationship.

In Chapter 10 of the gospel of John, Jesus describes himself as The Good Shepherd. He says of the relationship between himself and his sheep, *"I am the good shepherd; I know my sheep and my sheep know me...they will listen to my voice..."* (John 10:14,16a NIV). To be devoted followers of Jesus, we must know him. It is just as ridiculous to say you are a devoted follower of a Jesus you don't know as it would be to claim you are devoted to a spouse you don't know.

Devotion to Jesus **trusts**. Devotion rests on the solid foundation of real confidence in Jesus. Why do you suppose Jesus spent so much time in his teaching ministry addressing the issue of worry? Worry is evidence of distrust. In order to be devoted to Jesus, we must trust him.

If we trust Jesus, we will be faithful. He will have our exclusive allegiance. We will abide peacefully in him, without worry. Christ tells us in John 15 that we are to abide in him as branches abide (are attached to and dependent on) the vine. *"I am the vine; you are the branches. If you remain in me and I in you, you will bear much fruit; apart from me you can do nothing."* (John 15:5 NIV)

This kind of faithful allegiance again harkens back to the illustration of marriage. One of my parishioners tells me a story

I expect may sound familiar to many. As often happens with children, his sons tried to pit Mom against Dad in hopes of getting what they wanted. My friend sat his sons down and explained to them that if they were trying to divide Mom and Dad, they were playing a losing game. Mom and Dad were in a covenant relationship. They were inseparably joined. Any attempt the boys might make to separate them from one another was therefore destined to fail.

Don't try to separate a devoted disciple from Jesus. It is just not possible. The devoted disciple of Jesus trusts him and is so joined to him that nothing can sever the relationship of trust. Worry is overcome completely. The devoted disciple is so devoted to walking with Jesus that they are open to risk — even the loss of life or the breaking of family relationships. That is what Jesus was referring to in the center part of the scripture that opened this chapter (Matthew 10: 34-36) when he said, *"Do not suppose that I have come to bring peace to the earth. I did not come to bring peace, but a sword. For I have come to turn a man against his father, a daughter against her mother, a daughter-in-law against her mother-in-law — a man's enemies will be the members of his own household."* Certainly, family strife is not what God desires, but he warns us that it is a possible consequence of totally trusting in Jesus in radical allegiance and devotion.

Devotion to Jesus **remains.** The radical, exclusive allegiance referred to above is marked by eternal faithfulness. If forced to choose, we always choose him — no matter who is asking. We are so aligned with him that we are one with him. And this is precisely what Jesus prays for us. *"... I pray also for those who will believe in me through [the disciples'] message, that all of them may be one, Father, just as you are in me and I am in you. May they also be in us so that the world may believe that you have sent me. I have given them the glory that you gave me, that they may be one as we are one: I in them and you in me. May they be brought to complete unity to let the world know that you sent me and have loved them even as you have loved me.* (John 17:20-23, NIV)

Just as it is with the illustration of marriage where we "leave and cleave" (Genesis 2:24 KJV) and promise to stay together " 'til death do us part," so it is with the disciple's devotion to Jesus. Going back to the scripture reference at the beginning of the chapter, Jesus says, *"If the head of the house has been called Beelzebul, how much more the members of his household!"* (v. 25b) In other words, even when Jesus is accused of being Beelzebul (the Devil), we remain faithful. Whatever Jesus is called, we will also be. How did the Pharisees treat Jesus' disciples when they were seeking to put Jesus to death? The same way they treated him.

Devotion to Jesus **acknowledges.** Jesus clearly lets us know that if we are devoted to him, we acknowledge him before others, *"Whoever acknowledges me before others, I will also acknowledge before my Father in heaven. But whoever disowns me before others, I will disown before my Father in heaven."* (Matthew 10:32 NIV) We are never ashamed of bearing the name of Jesus. On the contrary, we look for ways to publicly proclaim the name of Jesus in a praiseworthy manner. Just as it is horrible to see husbands and wives publicly humiliate and denigrate one another, so also in our relationship with Jesus. If we love him, we want to represent him to others in a positive light.

Devotion to Jesus **obeys.** Devotion is expressed in full surrender and respect. Jesus stated this in a very straightforward manner in John 14 (NIV), *"If you love me, keep my commands."* (v. 15), *"Whoever has my commands and keeps them is the one who loves me. The one who loves me will be loved by my Father, and I too will love them and show myself to them."* (v. 21), and *"Anyone who loves me will obey my teaching. My Father will love them, and we will come to them and make our home with them."* (v. 23) It is impossible, therefore, to claim to be a devoted disciple who is unwilling to obey his commands.

Devotion to Jesus **sacrifices.** Certainly, Jesus sacrificed his very life for us, so our own devotion to him should be self-sacrificing when necessary, always choosing Christ over ourselves. Jesus' cross was not because of his own criminal conviction but rather for the benefit of others. So our own sacrifice is to be for the benefit of others. Again, Christ himself is our example, *"Anyone who loves their father or mother more than me is not worthy of me; anyone who loves their son or daughter more than me is not worthy of me. Whoever does not take up their cross and follow me is not worthy of me. Whoever finds their life will lose it, and whoever loses their life for my sake will find it."* (Matthew

24:37-39 NIV) and *"The reason my Father loves me is that I lay down my life—only to take it up again."* (John 10:17 NIV). In these words, Jesus is helping his disciples know the magnitude of their own sacrifice.

Devotion to Jesus **cares.** Our own devotion to Jesus is demonstrated by complete service to Christ and our genuine, sacrificial service to others. What was Jesus' response when he saw others who were harassed and downtrodden? Compassion. So should ours be. Caring for others is caring for Jesus. Remember Jesus' teaching regarding the sheep and the goats?

> *"Then the King will say to those on his right, 'Come, you who are blessed by my Father; take your inheritance, the kingdom prepared for you since the creation of the world. For I was hungry and you gave me something to eat, I was thirsty and you gave me something to drink, I was a stranger and you invited me in, I needed clothes and you clothed me, I was sick and you looked after me, I was in prison and you came to visit me.'*
>
> *"Then the righteous will answer him, 'Lord, when did we see you hungry and feed you, or thirsty and give you something to drink? When did we see you a stranger and invite you in, or needing clothes and clothe you? When did we see you sick or in prison and go to visit you?'*
>
> *"The King will reply, 'Truly I tell you, whatever you did for one of the least of these brothers and sisters of mine, you did for me.'* (Matthew 25: 34-40 NIV)

Jesus commands us to value the interests of others above our own, to love them as we love ourselves, just as he did. He came into this relationship with us not to be served, but to serve. Wow!

If this is what devotion looks like, how do we lead people to be like that? How can we, as disciple-makers, foster that kind of devotion? Let's look once again to our example disciple-maker, Jesus.

First, devotion must be fostered through **relationship**. Jesus invested in relationship with his disciples. As we referred to in the previous chapter, much of what happens in the West in the name of "discipling" is done through lesson and lecture in Bible studies, Sunday School or from the pulpit. Information is imparted, but little or no opportunity is there for accountability. If we are to expect the disciples we are making to mature in the devotion we've been defining, it cannot happen outside of relationships deep enough to include accountability. In our Palmwood Church community gatherings, we have chosen to regularly make time to ask one another, "How have you applied last week's teaching?" I expect that is pretty rare, but it shouldn't be if we are really about making disciples.

We've already established that devotion to someone cannot exist without a relationship with that person. It is also true that devotion is fostered through relationship. Not only do they need to know Jesus, they need to be in relationship with people who are already in love with our Lord.

I love how Paul puts this on display with his faith-son Timothy. He even articulates it in his second letter to him: *I thank God, whom I serve, as my forefathers did, with a clear conscience, as night and day I constantly remember you in my prayers. Recalling your tears, I long to see you, so that I may be filled with joy. I have been reminded of your sincere faith, which first lived in your grandmother Lois and in your mother Eunice and, I am persuaded, now lives in you also. For this reason I remind you to fan into flame the gift of God, which is in you through the laying on of my hands. For God did not give us a spirit of timidity, but a spirit of power, of love and of self-discipline.* (2 Timothy 1:3-7) Paul had a relationship with the whole family. Paul knew them and he also knew their faith story. He held Timothy in his heart as a son (1 Timothy 1:18; 2 Timothy 2:1). He walked with him long enough to witness the growth of his faith. He earned the right to give him counsel. Which brings us to the next thing on our list.

Devotion is fostered through **wise counsel**. In relationship, we give godly guidance. We must be willing to ask our maturing disciples, "Would Jesus handle that situation that way?." If the answer is negative, we need to help our new disciple with wise counsel from the scriptures. Life is the curriculum, but the Scriptures are the textbook (Hebrews 4:12). We use it within the relationship to teach. We use it to address change. We use it to help them grow — to fan the right things into flame, as Paul puts it. The Word of God is given for this (2 Timothy 3:16-17). The wise counsel of a friend is a beautiful thing and it fosters growth in the devotion of the recipient (Proverbs 27:9). If we have invested in their lives, we will have built a level of trust that lets us speak into their lives in a way that superficial relationships cannot.

Devotion is also fostered by **example**. How can we expect something we are unwilling to seek in our own lives? Besides the disciple making example of Jesus, we have the example of the apostle Paul who admonished the Corinthian believers to *"Follow my example, as I follow the example of Christ."* (1Corinthians 11:1), and to the Philippians *"Whatever you have learned or received or heard from me, or seen in me—put it into practice.* (Philippians 4:9) If we are to teach, we must model.

Spiritual disciplines (spiritual habits) of all sorts are best cultivated in relationship with accountability and example. If we expect our new disciple to deepen their prayer life, for example, we could give them a good book to read on prayer; but, how much better is it to kneel beside them and pray *with* them? Perhaps even read the book together, discuss it, and then work together to apply its principles. If someone has asked me to help them design a spiritual retreat, I don't send them a list of websites on the subject; rather, I invite them to join me for a few days away. Devotion is grown in life-on-life contact where we exemplify what is being taught.

We should also be willing to allow accountability to work both ways. In a good disciple making relationship, the student should be able to question his teacher, especially if circumstances don't look just right. Have you ever been reminded of your own teaching by one of your children? Humbling, but appropriate, when done respectfully!

I knew a family who was working with their children on table manners. A few basic manners were set forth and reminders were given. The "penalty" for breaking the rules was that the offender had to leave the table and go stand in the kitchen for the slow count of ten. The father shared how silly he and his wife felt when they had to stand in the kitchen! This is a trivial example, but the principle applies. We should not expect more from our new disciples than we are willing to strive to do ourselves, and we should expect to not only make them accountable to us, but to be accountable to them.

Last, becoming a devoted disciple takes **practice**. Just like anything else valuable in life, good practice makes perfect. It is not enough to know (in our head) the Christian Faith, we must also live it out. Obviously, there can be no example (above) without practice. We grow – we improve in the practice of our Faith – the more we live it out. Paul instructs the Philippians to do so (Philippians 4:8-9). Many of these practices we commonly call "spiritual disciplines": Worship, Celebration, Gratitude, Sabbath, Contemplation, Journaling, Retreat, Prayer, Simplicity, Solitude, Service, Hospitality and many more. They are spiritual habits that consistently draw us closer (more devoted) to God as we put them into practice.

Remember grace. Our brand new disciples will learn, but they will also make mistakes. Part of our job is to be there to catch them and remind them that failure is normal. Mistakes are an opportunity to learn. Because we have been given grace, grace must be extended.

To summarize, every good Hebrew in Jesus' day understood what it meant to be a disciple of a Rabbi (teacher). In his study, *The Dust of the Rabbi*[4], teacher Ray Vander Laan notes that the ultimate goals of the disciple were:

- to know what the Rabbi knows,
- to do what the Rabbi does,
- to be like the Rabbi.

That is exactly what it means to be a devoted disciple of our Rabbi, Jesus.

---

4   *The Dust of the Rabbi*, Zondervan, 2006.

Questions for Reflection and Application:

1. Are you *committed* to Christ or are you *devoted*? How do you know (what is the evidence)? Is your "relationship" with Christ driven by an agenda or is it really a growing love relationship?

2. Stop and think about one or two really good, godly marriages you have witnessed. What evidences of love and devotion do you see? Read Paul's description in Ephesians 5:21-33. Could you describe your own relationship with Jesus using terms from a good marriage? Why or why not?

3. If the kind of devotion to Jesus we are describing in this chapter knows, trusts, remains, acknowledges, obeys, sacrifices, and cares, in what ways is your own devotion to Jesus marked by the above traits? In which of these do you need to grow?

4. Consider Paul's disciple making relationship with Timothy. Take a moment and identify the people who have been like a "Paul" to you in life. If you can't think of anyone, pray and ask God to lead you to someone who can be your "Paul."

5. In what way are you being a "Paul" to someone else? If you are a mature believer and have no one in whom you are investing, make a list of two or three people you might invite into this kind of relationship.

CHAPTER THREE
A Disciple is Devoted to Jesus' People, the Church

Therefore, brothers and sisters, since we have confidence to enter the Most Holy Place by the blood of Jesus, by a new and living way opened for us through the curtain, that is, his body, and since we have a great priest over the house of God, let us draw near to God with a sincere heart and with the full assurance that faith brings, having our hearts sprinkled to cleanse us from a guilty conscience and having our bodies washed with pure water. Let us hold unswervingly to the hope we profess, for he who promised is faithful. And let us consider how we may spur one another on toward love and good deeds, not giving up meeting together, as some are in the habit of doing, but encouraging one another—and all the more as you see the Day approaching. (Hebrews 10:19-25)

They devoted themselves to the apostles' teaching and to fellowship, to the breaking of bread and to prayer. (Acts 2:42)

The second part of our definition of a disciple is one who is devoted to Jesus' followers, the church. When we talk about "going to church" in North America, we usually mean going to a certain building, perhaps decorated with a cross and stained glass, and most often with a sign that has the word "church" in the name. The definition of church for legal purposes such as tax-exemption or incorporation, is an organization. That's because neither the state nor the IRS recognizes the true definition of the church.

One of my favorite memories from Sunday School during my childhood is a song we sang:

I am the church! You are the church!
We are the church together!
All who follow Jesus,
all around the world!
Yes, we're the church together!
The church is not a building;
the church is not a steeple;
the church is not a resting place;
the church is a people.[5]

This song conveys a simple but mandatory truth: the church of Jesus is a people, a community, a family — not a building or

---

[5] Richard K. Avery, Donald S. Marsh Words © 1972 Hope Publishing Company

organization. Nowhere in the Bible will you find a building or an organization called "the church." When the Bible refers to the church, the reference is always to a people— a community of believers.

Del Tagget, in his video series, *Truth Project*[6], recognizes three kinds of community. **God** is, has always been, and always will be, in community — Father, Son, and Holy Spirit. **The family** is a community — husband, wife, and children. And **the church** is a community made up of the family of believers. The church, so defined, is the family to which a disciple of Jesus is devoted.

Remember the difference between being *committed* and being *devoted*. Commitment is made with the head and is agenda-driven. Devotion comes from the heart and is driven by relationship. A disciple is *devoted* to the church, not simply committed. The writer of Hebrews gives us a good description of church community in the scripture passage which opens the chapter.

When we celebrate the Lord's Table together, we often refer to Christ's sacrifice being "once for all." This passage is what we are referring to when we make that statement. You see, at the moment when Christ died on the cross, there was a great earthquake. That earthquake tore the curtain of the Temple that separated the Holy of Holies from the Holy Place completely in two — top to bottom. This opened access to the very presence of God to all believers. Up to this time, the Holy of Holies had been the

---

6　*The Truth Project*, Focus on the Family/Coldwater Media, 2007 dwelling place of God and entrance into it was restricted to the high priest alone, once a year, and then only after a prescribed series of cleansing rituals had been performed. The high priest had to go into the presence of God to offer sacrifices on behalf of the people to atone for their sins. The torn curtain was a powerful and unmistakable symbol of what Christ's sacrifice did for us — made it possible for us to be cleansed from our sins and allowed us to enter the very presence of God. God wanted to make sure that every Jew (and now, every Christ-follower) understood this. This access is what the writer of Hebrews is referring to when he says, *"...since we have confidence to enter the Most Holy Place by the blood of Jesus, by a new and living way opened for us through the curtain, that is, his body, and since we have a great priest over the house of God, let us draw near to God with a sincere heart and with the full assurance that faith brings, having our hearts sprinkled to cleanse us from a guilty conscience and having our bodies washed with pure water."* (Hebrews 10:19-22) Because of Jesus' sacrifice, we can have confidence in our ability to enter into the very presence of God, washed clean from our sins by the *very* blood of Jesus.

Exactly what does devotion to Jesus' people, the church, look like today?

This devotion looks like having confidence in God together. *"Therefore, brothers and sisters, since we have confidence to enter the Most Holy Place by the blood of Jesus, by a new and living way opened for us through the curtain, that is, his body,"* (v. 19-20) When the body of Christ is together in one place, there inevitably exists a spectrum of degrees of confidence in God. There are those who may not yet be believers, and there are those who have been believers for a long, long time, and everything in between. Because we are a body made up of fallen creatures who are working to become more like Christ, we fall all along this continuum at any given time. How many of us have desired God to answer a specific prayer but just weren't sure he would? Most, I'll venture. When we come into a community of believers, we can be assured that there will be those who have confidence when ours is weak. When we struggle with our faith, there are others who can come alongside to help and support us. The confidence of community is unwavering.

Devotion looks like drawing near to God together. *"... let us draw near to God with a sincere heart..."* (v. 22a) The Bible never refers to us individually as the bride of Christ. It is the church that is referred to as Christ's bride. While he certainly loves us individually, it is together that he loves us as his bride! When it comes to worship, there is just something special and sweet about corporate worship. We may, and should, have private times of worship where we pray, read scripture, and listen to or sing worship songs. But there remains something unique about the experience of gathering together in the shared experience of worshipping God as a family.

Devotion looks like having assurance of faith together. *"... and with the full assurance that faith brings...,"* (v. 22a) Looking back toward confidence, these two attributes go hand in hand. I am reminded of the story Jesus told in the second chapter of Mark where Jesus was in a house performing miracles of healing. An invalid man could not get inside. What did his friends do? They carried their friend up onto the roof, dug a hole through the roof, and lowered the man on his mat right down in front of Jesus! What a story! We aren't sure how the homeowner felt about the hole in his roof; we aren't told. The invalid's friends, however, were so convinced of Jesus' compassionate power that they did whatever it would take — and that is just what happened. The Bible tells us that Jesus was moved by the faith of those friends and the man was indeed set free. What an example of faith in community!

Devotion looks like practicing confession and cleansing together. *"...having our hearts sprinkled to cleanse us from a guilty conscience and having our bodies washed with pure water."* (v. 22b) James 5 deals with this. In the Western church if there is confession of sin, it is usually because there is something written out in the bulletin or prayer book for us to recite together. Rarely do we dare to say, "Friend, I am wrestling with something. I need to come to you and confess something so that I can be free from it." We don't want to "air our dirty laundry", in part because we do not trust each other in the church today. That's another problem we need to address. In many churches today, the environment does not feel trustworthy. There simply is no one with whom we feel we can be completely open. I've been in churches where the number one spiritual gift seems to be gossip. And that is not a gift from the Holy Spirit! In that environment, no one will be willing to confess if they must fear that whatever they say will be on the church grapevine within fifteen minutes. We need to cultivate an environment where we can trust one another and receive the cleansing of sin that we all need when we fall short.

Devotion looks like professing hope together. *"Let us hold unswervingly to the hope we profess, for he who promised is faithful."* (v. 23) When I use the word *hope* here, I mean expectation, not the weak meaning it has come to have in American English. We often use *hope* in reference to wishful thinking — *I hope it doesn't rain this afternoon*, or *I hope the Vikings win the Monday night football game.* That is not what I mean here. Biblical hope is confidence. I like to think of hope in the way my little German grandmother used it. Grandma was just shy of five feet tall, but she was the matriarch of our family, and when she said to me, "Johnny, I hope you'll be here by five o'clock for supper tonight," I knew she was *expecting* me to be there by five o'clock — if not ten minutes earlier. When I say we profess hope that Jesus will return or that my prayers will be answered, I mean that we *expect* these things to take place. We have confidence in Him. In the church then, when we are wavering in our faith, we can find the strength we need to profess real *hope* together.

Devotion looks like spurring one another on. *"And let us consider how we may spur one another on toward love and good deeds,"* (v. 24) In community, we urge one another to fully use our divine design — trying to outdo one another in loving and serving our community. We hear comments like, "Anyone can pray, but my brother, when you pray, I feel like heaven and earth move," or "I love it when we sing together, but when you sing, my sister, it's like the angels themselves join in." When we say these kinds of things, our divine design is showing. Use the gifts God has given you for the benefit of the community! We encourage one another to use our gifts, like Paul urged Timothy, *"I remind you to fan into flame the gift of God, which is in you through the laying on of my hands."* (2 Timothy 1:6) Spurring one another on can only happen in community.

Devotion looks like meeting together and encouraging one another. *"...not giving up meeting together, as some are in the habit of doing, but encouraging one another—and all the more as you see the Day approaching."* (v. 25) Meeting together is self-explanatory. This verse is certainly talking about worship, but it is also talking about life groups, small groups, study groups, or whatever similar term with which you are familiar. Gathering together in a large group for worship is important, but it is also important to gather in our homes. In today's world, one of the greatest tools we have for connecting people to Jesus is our dinner table. There may be no better place to foster relationships, intimacy and encouragement of one another. Honestly, based on our culture and all the "privacy fences" people put up to keep the world out, when you invite the world to your dinner table, that speaks volumes. It gives a great opportunity for the intimate sharing of Jesus together.

Devotion looks like learning from the Word together. *"They devoted themselves to the apostles' teaching and to the fellowship, to the breaking of bread and to prayer."* (Acts 2:42) It's important to note that the early Christians did not have the New Testament as we know it. They had what we call the Old Testament (it was in Hebrew and the books were in a different order, but it was comprised of the same scriptures). They were quickly recognizing that the teaching of the apostles (those who had been with Jesus) was also inspired and authoritative. Hence their devotion to the apostles' teaching. That teaching brought the Old Testament into focus, recognizing Jesus as their Messiah. That teaching instructed them on how to live and how to advance the rule and reign of Jesus among the peoples. That teaching was life-changing. These characteristics are still true for us today. If we are devoted to Jesus, we'll be devoted to the Old and New Testaments as the authoritative Word of God. We study the Word together, wrestling to understand and apply it rightly under the continuous influence of the Holy Spirit.

Devotion looks like being and working together. "*They devoted themselves to the apostles' teaching and to the fellowship, to the breaking of bread and to prayer.*" (Acts 2:42) There's an important word missing from many English translations of this verse — the word "the." In the Greek, there is a definite article. Luke here writes about *the* fellowship, not just a gathering based in affinity. The object of this devotion was the group, the people, the family. These were people in precious relationship with each other. These were people who were on a mission together — to spread the kingdom rule and reign of Jesus by making more disciples. This is the very essence of our chapter

— being devoted to Jesus' people! When we are in a vibrant, Christ-centered relationship with each other, our devotion is not just to our common task, but to each other.

Devotion looks like praying together. "*...to the breaking of bread and to prayer.*" (Acts 2:42b) Of course we should pray together as a body as part of our worship gatherings, but devotion to the community means going beyond this. It's not just going through a prayer list as a group, or sharing printed prayers, but about going to one another and lifting one another up concerning specific, personal needs. It means going beyond the often trite, "*I'll be praying for you,*" to "*Let's pray together right now.*" It's about praying *with* each other, not just *for* each other.

Devotion looks like eating meals and sharing Communion together. "*...to the breaking of bread and to prayer.*" (Acts 2:42b) Did you know that you are allowed to celebrate The Lord's Table in your own homes? I know that in some church traditions, only ordained clergy are allowed to administer the Lord's Table, but I do not see that in scripture. It is my opinion that any believer can celebrate the Lord's Table wherever believers are gathered. The Lord gave the simple direction that The Lord's Table was to be celebrated "in remembrance of him." (See Luke 22:19 KJV and 1 Corinthians 11:23-26 KJV)

This list can be expanded further when we add the description of this devotion from Acts 2:42, printed at the beginning of the chapter. Learning from the Word (apostolic teaching), loving the fellowship of the saints, praying and interceding, and breaking bread together – which would certainly have included communion ("whenever you gather together") but clearly also meant sharing meals together on a regular basis as family.

As you look at these things: having confidence in God, drawing near to God, having assurance of faith, practicing confession and knowing we are cleansed, having hope, spurring one another on by our divine design, meeting together, encouraging one another, learning together, praying together, eating and sharing communion together — these are the things the world yearns for, and they are the divine design of God's community called the church. There is no other group — no other organization as equipped as we are to give these things to the world. God gave us the church! It's our gift! He gave us spiritual gifts to be used for the common good. Yes, some can be practiced individually for valuable purposes, but they are designed to be used to put Jesus on display to the world. The "you" Jesus was referring to in his teaching, *"you are the light of the world"* (Matthew 5:14a) is not an individual light. It is plural. The church as a community is the light of the world! When the world sees how we love one another, how we pray together, how we encourage one another, how we have hope, and all of the ways we are devoted to one another, they will know we are his disciples. When two or three are gathered together, something that can only happen in community takes place. I certainly believe that Jesus is with each of us individually wherever we go in the world, but I also believe that there are things that are reserved for God to do in community. We're designed for this. Before evil entered the world, there was only one thing God said was not good — it was not good for man to be alone. The nature of God is community — Father, Son, and Holy Spirit. You and I are made in his image.

So how do we foster this devotion to the community of Christ as part of our disciple making? For those answers, we can turn to the Bible, the text written by the Author of Community. There are over fifty "one anothers" in the New Testament to guide us. Many of these can be gathered into categories, so I have tried to compile a list of scripture references that represent each of the major guidelines for developing community. Remember that this list is not at all exhaustive!

One caution before we begin our list. Those you are trying to disciple must be invited into a relationship, both with you and with your faith community, where they can observe and experience the "one anothers" of Scripture first hand. Many people in the Western Church seem to have the idea that you have to "believe like us before you can belong with us." I think that is exactly the opposite of what the scripture teaches. I think drawing people into the community so they can learn what it means to believe is the biblical example. Remember when Jesus invited his twelve disciples into his rabbinical community, how many were believers in Jesus as the Messiah and Savior? How many were saved? The answer is zero. That's the pattern. I would highly recommend that you take a moment to review the Engel

Scale found in Chapter Two. Our disciple making work is to, in concert with the Holy Spirit, slide people along that scale. How then, do we proceed?

Love one another. *"A new command I give you: Love one another. As I have loved you, so you must love one another."* (John 13:34) People learn to be devoted to one another when they experience us loving one another. Remember that Jesus said this was how the world would know that we belonged to him — how we love one another. Nearly 25% of the "one anothers" of the New Testament have something to do with how we love one another. Therefore, we need to be purposeful in showing that love is a decision, not a feeling, as Jesus did on the cross. This kind of love puts others before self — always working for their good. It's other-oriented — not seeking something in return. If there is a number one priority in our community, this is it.

Be at peace with one another. *"Salt is good, but if it loses its saltiness, how can you make it salty again? Have salt among yourselves, and be at peace with each other."* (Mark 9:50) Biblical peacemaking is something that does not come naturally to most of us. Most people deal with conflict in one of two ways — they either run away from it or they try to control it. Very few people actually work to resolve it. That is a skill that can be taught. It is a command of Jesus. We are called to be ministers of reconciliation. (2 Corinthians 5:18) Therefore, when people see us in the family of God living out this biblical peacemaking, it draws them in. Peacemaking is something we must teach and practice.

Welcome one another. *"Accept one another, then, just as Christ accepted you, in order to bring praise to God."* (Romans 15:7) Inviting and welcoming are both important, but they are not exactly the same. A welcoming community makes it apparent that we are happy to meet new people. We are because we know God's heart and we get excited about everything God wants to do in those lives. It's more than just shaking hands and saying, "Nice to meet you." It's a pervading spirit that makes people feel like part of the family.

This welcoming spirit is not to be just displayed in our worship gatherings, but in every aspect of our lives — including our homes. I have a neighbor who came to visit our house at our invitation shortly after we moved in. He remarked that in the twenty-some years their family had lived in that neighborhood, that was the first time he had been invited into what was now our house. Our culture is simply not "neighborly" anymore. Our homes and our kitchen tables are some of our strongest tools for drawing people into our community. We need to be intentional about being welcoming into our worship gatherings, our small groups, special events and our homes.

Care for one another. *"...so that there should be no division in the body, but that its parts should have equal concern for each other."* (1 Corinthians 12:25) Caring for one another should be both reactive (when there is an emergency, for instance) and proactive. We can, and should be, looking around us for those who need care and brainstorming about what it might look like for you and I to address that need. Because this care is always directly tied to the love we have, it strives for the heart not just to alleviate the circumstances.

Be patient with one another. *"Be completely humble and gentle; be patient, bearing with one another in love."* (Ephesians 4:2) Patience seems to be at an all time low all around us. Just take a drive on a local busy highway at rush hour and you'll see what I mean. Real patience can have a huge impact on people. In a world filled with stress, overburdened schedules and political sniping, authentic forbearance — especially with those who are in the process of maturing — is an expression of love.

Serve one another. *"You, my brothers and sisters, were called to be free. But do not use your freedom to indulge the flesh; rather, serve one another humbly in love."* (Galatians 5:13) That is self-explanatory. If we are a loving community that truly puts others and their needs ahead of ourselves, then serving is a regular part of our life together. Serving one another becomes so "normal" that it then also spills over, outside the community of faith, in loving service to the world as well, and the world recognizes it as different and desirable.

Forgive one another. *"Bear with each other and forgive one another if any of you has a grievance against someone. Forgive as the Lord forgave you."* (Colossians 3:13) Forgiveness, like love, is a major priority for God's people, but it is one thing the world does not do well — and in some cases — actually considers a weakness. Within the community of faith, forgiveness is a command. Jesus' people are not allowed to withhold forgiveness — ever. Most believers who do not forgive fail to do so because they do not know how, but this is a skill that can be learned. It is part of the process of peacemaking. Even within the church, we tend to tell people that the Bible teaches that we have to forgive, but the church often fails to teach us exactly what that means, what it looks like, or how to do it. Dr. Ken Sande teaches four essential promises of forgiveness that are helpful here:

- I will not dwell on this incident.
- I will not bring this incident up and use it against you.
- I will not talk to others about this incident.
- I will not allow this incident to stand between us or hinder our personal relationship.[7]

(For more information, see *www.www.Peacemaker.net* "*The Four Promises of Forgiveness*") When forgiveness is practiced, it's amazing how this feature of the Church begins to change hearts and attitudes.

Comfort one another. "*Therefore encourage one another with these words.*" (1 Thessalonians 4:18) Comfort. Everyone needs

---

[7] Ken Sande, *The Peacemaker: A Biblical Guide to Resolving Personal Conflict*, Grand Rapids: Baker Books, 2004.

it from time to time. Paul teaches us to comfort people in the same ways we have experienced comfort, *"Praise be to the God and Father of our Lord Jesus Christ, the Father of compassion and the God of all comfort, who comforts us in all our troubles, so that we can comfort those in any trouble with the comfort we ourselves receive from God."* (2 Corinthians 1:3-4) It's easy to see how this level of comforting becomes a natural trait of a truly loving, caring, serving community of faith.

Provoke one another towards love and good deeds. *"And let us consider how we may spur one another on toward love and good deeds, not giving up meeting together, as some are in the habit of doing, but encouraging one another—and all the more as you see the Day approaching."* (Hebrews 10:24-25) When a community has a culture of outdoing one another in loving acts and good deeds, it is contagious. Here, the Church pays attention to each one's divine design and urges them to minister according to it. When someone comes into the community and sees us encouraging one another in those "divine design" aspects of ourselves to do this or that, it draws them in.

Confess to one another. *"Therefore confess your sins to each other and pray for each other so that you may be healed. The prayer of a righteous person is powerful and effective."* (James 5:16) There is something powerful about confession — not a printed recitation from the Sunday bulletin, but real, heart-felt confession of sin within safe relationships where there is mutual love and accountability. Again, a skill that can be taught.[8]

Teach and admonish one another. *"Let the message of Christ dwell among you richly as you teach and admonish one another with all wisdom through psalms, hymns, and songs from the Spirit, singing to God with gratitude in your hearts."* (Colossians 3:16) Finally, here is a fulfillment of the Great Commission itself to "teach them to obey everything I have commanded you." Remember that this is not just passing on information and facts, but teaching toward full obedience. By pairing the teaching here with admonishment — warning — we're teaching Jesus' commands while warning about both the consequences of disobedience and how the non-believing world may respond to our new life in Christ.

When people come into our church family and they see us loving one another, being at peace, welcoming one another, caring for each other, being patient, serving one another, forgiving each other, comforting each other, provoking each other toward good deeds, confessing to one another, receiving forgiveness, and teaching and admonishing one another so that we all grow, there is a draw that is hard to resist. They realize that we are not just a bunch of grumpy old people who are thumping the Bible and voting a certain way. They find out that we love each other and we actually intend to live by that. We are a community, a family, a body where every part has a role to play. We are not

---

[8] For further detail, see https://rw360.org/seven-as-of-a-biblical-confession/

A Disciple is Devoted to Jesus' People, the Church

a complete body unless we are together. We need one another. As we walk through life together we learn better how the pieces are designed to fit together. Iron sharpens iron, and yes that produces sparks, but that is why we have peace with one another. We depend on each other as we learn to be the community that God has designed us to be.

Questions for Reflection and Application:

1. 1 Peter 2:9-10 says this about the church: *"But you are a chosen people, a royal priesthood, a holy nation, God's special possession, that you may declare the praises of him who called you out of darkness into his wonderful light. Once you were not a people, but now you are the people of God; once you had not received mercy, but now you have received mercy."* How does knowing the church is the gathering of believers (the people of God), change your view of "church"? How does this truth change the target of your devotion — are you devoted to an organization? An agenda? A building? Or a people?

2. Review the list of what devotion to the community of Jesus' people, the church, looks like (including that from Acts 2:42), and measure your own experience by it. In which of these areas are you currently investing? In which areas might you need to become more devoted?

3. Carefully and thoughtfully look over the list of "one anothers." How have these traits of the church impacted you? In which of these areas is your faith community strong? In which areas might they be encouraged to grow? How are you personally participating in them? In which areas might you need to grow?

CHAPTER FOUR
A Disciple is Devoted to Jesus' Mission– His Passion

'Now get up and stand on your feet. I have appeared to you to appoint you as a servant and as a witness of what you have seen and will see of me. I will rescue you from your own people and from the Gentiles. I am sending you to them to open their eyes and turn them from darkness to light, and from the power of Satan to God, so that they may receive forgiveness of sins and a place among those who are sanctified by faith in me.'

"So then, King Agrippa, I was not disobedient to the vision from heaven. (Acts 26:16-19)

Thus begins the testimony of Paul to King Agrippa. Because he was a Roman citizen, Paul did not have to go through much of what he endured after being arrested. Paul chose to appeal his case all the way to Caesar, if possible, in order to take the message of the gospel as far up the chain of command as he could. That's devotion to Jesus' mission — his passion.

DISCIPLE MAKING

In Chapter Two, we introduced the concept of a three-fold definition of a disciple as described by my friends Tom Johnston and Mike Perkinson.[9] We spent Chapters Two and Three with the first two parts of that definition, which were that disciples were devoted to Christ and to his people, the Church. In this chapter, we will look at the third part of that definition — a disciple is devoted to Jesus' mission, which is his passion. Following the pattern established in the two previous chapters, we will first examine what Jesus' mission looks like, and then we will talk about how to instill that in his people.

Remember, Jesus commissioned his Church. We are to be obedient to his mission. American Christians tend to get on the "hamster wheel" of pet projects and spend their energy doing the same things over and over — but those things may *not* be Jesus' things. Take a look at the graphic on the next page. In Luke 4:14-22, Jesus defined his mission when he entered the synagogue, opened the scroll of the book of Isaiah, and read from what we now know as Chapter 61. This articulated exactly what he had been sent to do: preach the good news, proclaim freedom for the captives, recovery of sight for the blind, set free the oppressed, and proclaim the year of the Lord's favor (God's grace). We see, in examining Jesus' mission, that this is the very same mission he has commissioned his disciples to as well. It might be walked out a bit differently in our case than it was by the very Son of God, but the mission is the same!

---

[9] Tom Johnston and Mike Chong Perkinson, *The Organic Reformation: A New Hope for the Church in the West*, Manchester, NH: Praxis Media, 2012, pp. 70-71.

We see Paul is devoted to this mission, as he now stands before the Roman authorities, in this case King Agrippa. He is giving his testimony about the Damascus Road experience where Jesus met him. This was the turning point in Paul's life. He went from being a Pharisee, trying to stamp out what he deemed a threat to the Jewish faith by persecuting those who were following Jesus, to becoming a Jesus follower himself. Talk about a radical change! His certainly was a radical story of salvation. Standing before King Agrippa, Paul is sharing the experience of meeting Jesus and hearing directly from him. If you look at the chart, you will see that the mission Paul describes for himself closely parallels the mission Jesus articulated from the prophet Isaiah.

(Luke 4:14-22)	Paul (Acts 26:16-19)
Preach the good news	Be a servant and a witness
Proclaim freedom for the captives	Proclaim freedom for the captives
Recovery of sight for the blind	Open their eyes
Set free the oppressed	Turn them from the power of Satan to God — freeing the oppressed
Proclaim the year of the Lord's favor (God's grace)	Proclaim forgiveness of sins and a place among the sanctified (God's "set apart ones") — proclaiming God's grace

The same pattern is seen again in the gospels of Matthew and Luke when Jesus sends out the twelve and the seventy-two. He gives them essentially the same mission. They are told to preach the good news of the kingdom, heal the sick, and deliver the oppressed. (See Matthew 10:7-8, Luke 9:1-2 & Luke 10:8-9) This mission is for everyday Christians, just like it was for our Savior, just like it was for the Apostle Paul, and just like it was for the disciples sent out by Jesus. The word "Christian" means "one who is like Christ." Remember that Paul urged his "son in the faith", Timothy, to "imitate me as I imitate Christ." Jesus' earthly ministry emphasized both this mission and the discipling of those who would continue and expand it. After his resurrection, Jesus meets his disciples as they are gathered together and tells them that he is sending them out just as his Father had sent him out (John 20:19-23). Jesus' followers down through the ages are to carry out the very same mission: bring his authority to bear on the world thereby advancing his kingdom rule and reign, and continue to make more disciples who will do the same (Matthew 28:18-20; Mark 16:15-20). Jesus' disciples are devoted to this mission.

What does this devotion to Jesus' mission look like? First, let's take a moment to describe what it doesn't look like. Unfortunately, there are well-intentioned people who almost seem to bludgeon people with the gospel. In my view, this could be part of the reason many in the world today to view the Church with disdain. Some of us have failed to be kind and gracious witnesses. In some cases, I've seen people whose words and actions could be accurately described as just plain mean. Those people may be well-intentioned, but they are not being like Christ.

In order to fulfill Jesus' mission the way he intended, we must approach people with the right spirit. Effective sharing of the

A Disciple is Devoted to Jesus' Mission– His Passion

gospel of Jesus Christ cannot be an *us* versus *them* proposition. Sharing the gospel *must* be done in the right spirit, and that right spirit can be taught — remembering our own need of a Savior. We must remember that we too are sinners, fully and completely saved by Jesus Christ. Just as Jesus came in grace and truth, never compromising the truth, but sharing it with grace, so we must, never compromising the truth, share the truth with grace.

We are called to make mature disciples. Making mature disciples is the point of Jesus' words in what we call the Great Commission: *"All authority in heaven and on earth has been given to me. Therefore go and make disciples of all nations, baptizing them in the name of the Father and of the Son and of the Holy Spirit, and teaching them to obey everything I have commanded you."* (Matthew 28:18-20) Before he left in a cloud of glory to be taken to the right hand of the Father, it is what he told us we must do. Referring back to the Engel Scale (see Chapter 1, Figure 1), we see that the process of making disciples begins before a person makes a commitment to Jesus Christ and we nudge them along the journey to the point of conversion. After they have surrendered to Christ, we continue to nudge them along the journey to maturity where they really understand who they are in Christ and begin themselves to make disciples. Fully mature disciples always make disciples. They are not mature until they do. As you see in the Great Commission, Jesus called us to make disciples. We cannot quit the process at the point of conversion — "put a notch in our belts" — and move on. We must mentor disciples to maturity.

We are called to be a servant. Referring back to Paul's words in his testimony printed at the beginning of the chapter, Paul clearly says that our mission is to serve those around us (*...as a servant...*) (v. 16b*).* If we are truly striving to be in Christ's likeness and devoted to his mission, we must serve those around us. It is a humbling experience to be called by God to serve a world that doesn't even know him yet. Again, we must keep in mind from whence we came, and this is even more true for pastors and other Christian leaders, for we will be judged even more strictly (James 3:1). Advanced schooling is important, but we must never lead with titles and position. Remember that Jesus said, *"The greatest among you will be your servant."* (Matthew 23:11). We must be other-oriented and self-sacrificing like Christ. This is the heart attitude that leads us to serve others.

We are called to be a witness. *"...and as a witness of what you have seen and will see of me."* (v. 16b). Some Christians fear witnessing for Christ. When this is true, it is because they do not understand what it means to be a witness. They make statements like, "I just don't know the Bible well enough to be a good witness." To be a good witness, you do not have to know the Bible well; you have to know Jesus! A witness simply tells people what they know; what they have seen. If you witness an accident and are interviewed by the police, the officer will ask you to tell what you saw. The officer doesn't expect you to be an expert in all aspects of the physics of the crash or the laws that might have been broken. You are simply asked to tell what you saw. All you need to know to be a good witness for Jesus, then, is the answer to the questions, "Who is Jesus to you? What has he done in your life?" You are the expert on your own story. No one can refute that. It is your own story. Our devotion to Jesus' mission leads us to consistently tell those we meet what Jesus has done for us, how he has answered our prayers, and what we have seen him do.

We are called to open their eyes. *"...I am sending you to them to open their eyes..."* (v 17b-18a). This is where the authority we have in Christ begins to take root. If you have surrendered to Christ as King of All Kings and Lord of All Lords, the Bible says that you are a child of God. God is the Ancient of Days and Jesus is the Crown Prince. If we are his children, what are we other than princes and princesses? We are part of the family. In Romans 8:29, Paul explains it this way, *"For those God foreknew he also predestined to be conformed to the image of his Son, that he might be the firstborn among many brothers and sisters."* We are part of God's family, and as such, we have the authority of the family.

This imperative to *"open their eyes"* is two-fold. It is both authoritative and tactical. If we are devoted to Christ's mission, then we will also *lovingly* (Remember — right spirit!) expose people's self-centeredness. We will be mirrors that reflect back what we see in them because the number one obstacle humanity has when it comes to the acceptance of the message of Jesus Christ is self. We will also help them become aware, if they are not, of their condition, of the fallenness of the world, and help them become cognizant of their choices. These are tactical, but at the same time, there is a spiritual component we must recognize. When "the gospel lightbulb" went on in your life, it was not because of the person who was witnessing to you, it was because the Holy Spirit was doing his work. The apostle Paul tells us that Satan blinds people to the light of the gospel (2 Corinthians 4:4). Only the Spirit can open such blind eyes. There is a spiritual component that is in response to intercessory prayer. Tactical actions are necessary. There are things we have to do. We sometimes pray and pray and wait for God to do something, but all that time, God may be sitting on his throne saying, *"Yes, but I am waiting to use you as my instrument to accomplish that task."* The actual opening of the eyes so that people see their condition is the Holy Spirit's job, but we have a partner role to play by his design in opening their eyes.

We are called to turn them away from Satan's dominion and to God's kingdom. *"...and turn them from darkness to light, and from the power of Satan to God,"* (v. 18a). As we work with the Holy Spirit to open their eyes, standing in the authority of who we are — Christ's ambassador and a redeemed child of God — we sever that tie and turn them away from Satan's dominion, power, control and kingship. From that bondage, we turn them to the Kingdom of God — his rule and reign. We sever the bonds of Satan's darkness and move them to the light of Christ. *"For he has rescued us from the dominion of darkness and brought us into the kingdom of the Son he loves,"* (Colossians 1:13) *"For you were once darkness, but now you* *are light in the Lord. Live as children of light."* (Ephesians 5:8) When that tipping point comes, we must then teach them about our next point — forgiveness.

We are called to teach them about forgiveness. *"... so that they may receive forgiveness of sins..."* (v. 18b). This essential truth is not only about the forgiveness we receive from God. It is also about the way we become a conduit of God's forgiveness to all our other relationships. In all my years of pastoral ministry, I've never had anyone who has been around the church for any length of time question whether or not we're supposed to forgive. People know that. What I've seen repeatedly is that they don't know *how* to do that. There are Christians who have been redeemed and forgiven by Jesus all around our country — probably all around the world — who are stuck because the church has never taught them how to release forgiveness to other people. That's part of the sequence. We teach them how to receive God's forgiveness, but then we need to teach them how to then allow that forgiveness to flow through them to reach others.

Global Advance's David Shibley uses an illustration that spoke to me in a season of my life when I was struggling with forgiveness. Picture the side of a house with a hose and a spigot. Now picture the spigot open wide and the handle broken off so that the flow of water through that spigot into the hose is at full pressure and no one can turn it off. That water is God's forgiveness. Now picture a nozzle at the end of that hose. You and I are that nozzle. If we are cinched down tight, the water stops where we are. If forgiveness cannot flow *through* us, it cannot flow *to* us.

In Matthew 6, right after Jesus teaches his disciples about prayer, he says these very scary words, *"For if you forgive other people when they sin against you, your heavenly Father will also forgive you. But if you do not forgive others their sins, your Father will not forgive your sins."* (Matthew 6:14-15). Now, a bit of personal theology: I don't think, at this point, Jesus is talking about the spigot. I think he is talking about the nozzle. I think he is talking about the day-to-day forgiveness that you and I, as believers, are supposed to walk in. We are supposed to be free in forgiveness and setting people free with forgiveness. I think he means that if we cinch off the nozzle of God's forgiveness flowing through us to others, we also impede the flow of the life and freedom of God's forgiveness to us.

Devotion to Jesus' mission looks like forgiveness because it rests on forgiveness. Think about it. The whole of the Christian faith comes down to that — forgiveness — the forgiveness of God in Jesus Christ toward us. That's why Paul says that our forgiveness must be just the way God forgives us in Jesus Christ (Ephesians 4:32). Christians are not allowed to shut down "the nozzle" of forgiveness. Therefore, how to forgive is something we must teach.

We are called to mentor them in their place among the sanctified. *"...and a place among those who are sanctified by faith in me."* (v. 18b) Now we draw them into the body of Christ and mentor them. What does this mentoring look like? It looks like making mature disciples, being a servant, being a witness, opening their eyes, turning them from Satan's dominion to God's kingdom, and teaching them about forgiveness as we teach them to take their place among the sanctified. As we discussed at length in the last chapter, this is our opportunity to show them what life in the community of Christ is like!

So how do we now foster that? Unsurprisingly, as we have discussed before, it is all done in relationship. Devotion to Jesus' mission cannot be taught from behind a lectern — not if you really want people to understand it. You have to take them by the hand and live it with them. They must see it on display.

We make disciple-makers. People come to church for many different reasons. Some come to spend time with friends, because their parents bring them, to be spiritually fed by the sermon, to enjoy the music, or for a host of other reasons, but the main reason we are *supposed* to be here is for the mission. When we gather together we need to disciple one another to be disciple-makers. So often when I talk to churches who are really not making disciples at all, the pastor or Board of Elders will ask, "So how do you do this?" What they seem to want is an A-B-C-D outline so they can teach or preach the steps in their meetings or messages. It doesn't work that way. Jesus spent three years discipling the twelve. That's the model he gave us. We need to live in relationship with those we are discipling, so that they can grow, and so that they can imitate us as we imitate Jesus. Sound familiar? That's the way it works. That's the way Jesus designed it. It's never been different. The American church is the one that's tried to make it an academic experience. To quote Dr. Phil, "How's that working for us?" Not so well, I fear. So let's get back to the relational model that Jesus gave us in the first place.

We give them opportunities to serve with us. The key here is the phrase *with us*. Churches are great at coming up with all kinds of ideas for ways you can serve and posting them in the bulletin, on flyers, or on their websites. That's wonderful as far as it goes, but most American churches do very poorly at connecting volunteers to mentors in those areas of service so that they can learn to serve in a way that produces fruit and honors Jesus. We need to serve together. How much better to recruit people according to their divine design and then intentionally disciple them in that area of ministry.

We practice real witnessing with them. Notice the word *with* is there again. I am convinced that people are afraid to witness for two primary reasons: 1) They don't understand what witnessing really is, and/or 2) They've never actually seen it. What they may have seen is someone standing on a soap box on a street corner somewhere, or someone grabbing unsuspecting strangers — tract in hand — and preaching *at* people rather than seeing someone simply engaging people in conversation about who Jesus is and telling what he has done for us. So we take them along and we show them what real witnessing is.

We ensure that they have critical awareness. We help them understand the Good News of Jesus Christ, but it's in comparison to the bad news of not having a relationship with Jesus Christ. We help them understand the consequences of this choice, not only for themselves, but so that they can share that with other people. Paul writes to the church at Colossae, *" Let the word of Christ dwell in you richly as you teach and admonish one another with all wisdom, and as you sing psalms, hymns and spiritual songs with gratitude in your hearts to God"* (Colossians 3:16). He also writes in his letter to the Thessalonians, *"Therefore encourage one another and build each other up, just as in fact you are doing"* (1 Thessalonians 5:11). A significant part of discipling others is to lovingly teach, encourage and also admonish them by the word of Christ. We reflect back their words and actions in light of Christ's example. We help them to be aware of where they are most like Christ and where growth is needed. We hold *one another* accountable.

We show them where each kingdom leads. People need to understand where they are heading. We show them that if they continue down the road they are on, there is an outcome — a destination — for them. We need to help them ask themselves, "Is this really the place I want to go?" John 3:19b-20 tells us that people actually love the darkness because they do not want their deeds exposed. (*...people loved darkness instead of light because their deeds were evil. Everyone who does evil hates the light, and will not come into the light for fear that their deeds will be exposed.*) This isn't supposed to be about exposing their dirty laundry though sometimes that happens. It is about setting them free. *The prudent see danger and take refuge, but the simple keep going and pay the penalty.* (Proverbs 22:3) We warn them because we love them.

We teach them what forgiveness means and how to forgive. In our church, we follow the Ken Sande's definition of forgiveness (refer back to Chapter 3, page 50). When we say, "I forgive you," there are four promises we are making to that person. If we cannot make those four promises, to say "I forgive you" is actually lying.[10] Forgiving is a skill that can be learned. We should be teaching this skill.

We draw them into the sanctified community. We invite them deeper into the kind of relationship we discussed in Chapter 3. It's all done in relationship. We make disciple-makers. We give them opportunities to serve and to witness with us. We ensure that they have critical awareness. We show them where each kingdom ultimately leads. We teach them about forgiveness and how to forgive, and we draw them into the sanctified community of believers.

A disciple is devoted to Jesus. A disciple is devoted to Jesus' people, the church. A disciple is devoted to Jesus' mission, his passion, but this is more than just desire. There is a vast difference between simple passion, and passion with Christ-centered devotion. His passion becomes our passion. Passion may drive someone, but it is often circumstantial and/or temporary. Passion with Christ-centered devotion is based upon an abiding relationship with the Savior. This makes all the difference. The disciple counts the cost. Jesus talked about this in the Gospel of Luke:

---

10   For more information on this definition and the four promises, see www.rw360.org.

A Disciple is Devoted to Jesus' Mission– His Passion

> *"As they were walking along the road, a man said to him, "I will follow you wherever you go."*
>
> *Jesus replied, "Foxes have holes and birds of the air have nests, but the Son of Man has no place to lay his head."*
>
> *He said to another man, "Follow me."*
>
> *But the man replied, "Lord, first let me go and bury my father."*
>
> *Jesus said to him, "Let the dead bury their own dead, but you go and proclaim the kingdom of God."*
>
> *Still another said, "I will follow you, Lord; but first let me go back and say good-by to my family."*
>
> *Jesus replied, "No one who puts his hand to the plow and looks back is fit for service in the kingdom of God."*
>
> (Luke 9:57-62)

Because a disciple is fully devoted to Jesus and is also devoted to Jesus' people (the Church), he or she is devoted to Jesus' mission. This devotion acts out of the love we have for the Savior, and it acts in concert with the Body of Christ as we share His priorities in reaching the world. When it comes to devotion to Jesus, we are either all in, or we are not in at all. We have talked about the Engel Scale, and I acknowledge that this is a process, but when it comes to the destination, we must be all in. You and I proclaim Jesus because we are fully and completely devoted to him.

Let me end this way, understanding that in the ancient Jewish mindset, all sacrifices were dead when they were offered. Hear the words of Paul to the Romans. *"Therefore, I urge you, brothers and sisters, in view of God's mercy, to offer your bodies as a living sacrifice, holy and pleasing to God—this is your true and proper worship. Do not conform to the pattern of this world, but be transformed by the renewing of your mind. Then you will be able to test and approve what God's will is—his good, pleasing and perfect will. For by the grace given me I say to every one of you: Do not think of yourself more highly than you ought, but rather think of yourself with sober judgment, in accordance with the faith God has distributed to each of you."* (Romans 12:1-3) The sacrifices of the Old Testament, being completely dead, could only be offered once. Paul is urging believers to continually offer their very bodies as living sacrifices to God — to be all in always! We are redeemed, and that is something to celebrate, but in and of ourselves, we are no big deal. We are simply fellow servants on this journey. We are willing, living sacrifices. Old Testament sacrifices could serve only once because they were dead. Living sacrifices are able to serve continuously. A disciple has to grow into this level of devotion, but mature disciples are "all in."

> Jesus, meet us where we are. It sometimes seems easier to be devoted to you and your people than it is to be devoted to your mission. Convict us where we need to be convicted, correct us where we need to be corrected, and empower us where we need to be empowered. Speak to us from

A Disciple is Devoted to Jesus' Mission– His Passion

your Word. Transform our hearts and minds. Impassion us. Where we have obstacles in our lives, whether self-inflicted and in need of forgiveness, or whether put there by others and in need of grace, grant us what we need to be free to walk in devoted obedience to your mission. Be our teacher and our guide as we follow wherever you lead. Amen.

Questions for Reflection and Application:

1. Review the graphic near the beginning of the chapter that details Jesus' mission (from Luke 4:14-21) and consider each of that mission's five components. In what ways have you experienced each of them in your own relationship with Jesus? How might you be called to fulfill each in your relationships with others? How are you conveying these things to those around you into whom you are investing as disciples?

2. Review the chart on page 51, this time focusing on Paul's mission (Acts 26:16-19). Who have been the people in your own life who have done these thing to/for you? In what ways is your church living them out today? In what ways are you personally living them out for the sake of others? What is the Holy Spirit whispering to you?

3. Reconsider the scripture reference we call The Great Commission. *"All authority in heaven and on earth has been given to me. Therefore go and make disciples of all nations, baptizing them in the name of the Father and of the Son and of the Holy Spirit, and teaching them to obey everything I have commanded you."* (Matthew 28:18-20). Consider how you are becoming Jesus' disciple. Who has come alongside you in your faith journey? Who has exemplified service to you? Who has demonstrated the power and simplicity of witnessing for Christ?

A Disciple is Devoted to Jesus' Mission– His Passion

Who is it that lovingly provides you with the critical awareness you need to grow? And for whom are you providing these things?

4. Prayerfully reflect on Romans 12:1-2 and Luke 9:57-62, both of which are printed near the end of the chapter. How does your own devotion to Jesus' mission measure up? Are you "all in"? How do you know?

CHAPTER FIVE
Disciples Make Disciples

You then, my son, be strong in the grace that is in Christ Jesus. And the things you have heard me say in the presence of many witnesses entrust to reliable people who will also be qualified to teach others. Join with me in suffering, like a good soldier of Christ Jesus. No one serving as a soldier gets entangled in civilian affairs, but rather tries to please his commanding officer. Similarly, anyone who competes as an athlete does not receive the victor's crown except by competing according to the rules. The hardworking farmer should be the first to receive a share of the crops. Reflect on what I am saying, for the Lord will give you insight into all this. (2 Timothy 2:1-7)

The graphic on the next page, adapted from Terry Walling's *leaderbreakthru.com,* is a good illustration of the point Paul was making to his disciple Timothy in his letter from which we have quoted above.

DISCIPLE MAKING

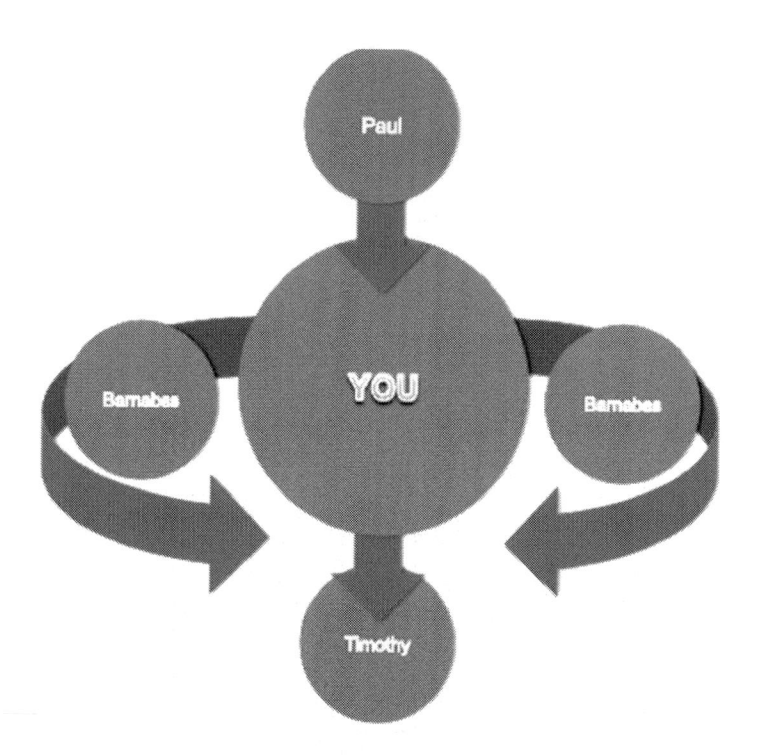

Paul is instructing his son in the faith Timothy. Paul, who was discipled by Jesus, and to some extent by Barnabas, poured into Timothy the way others had poured into him. And he says to Timothy: "the way I have poured into you is the way you should pour into other reliable people — so that they can disciple others also." Disciple making is a generational enterprise.

In every disciple's life there should be three kinds of relationships. Of course, we understand that when a disciple is brand new in the faith, it will take some time for this to fully develop, but as we mature this diagram should be a diagram of our lives as well. Each of us as disciples should have at least one "Paul" who is pouring into us (preferably more than one!). Those who know me well know that I have three men who regularly and consistently pour into my life — discipling me on an ongoing basis. We should also have "Timothy" relationships — people that we are pouring into. We do not have to wait for perfection, to earn a degree in theology, or to know everything about the Bible. We begin discipling as soon as we know enough to tell people about our Jesus. In disciple making it is less about *what* you know than it is about *Who* you know. Yes, we do need a basic understanding of what God has done for us through Jesus Christ, but to begin making disciples, it is most important for us to know Jesus ourselves and to be able to pass on what he has done for us. As we grow in the faith, understand more, and have more life experience with Jesus, we should be able to pour into one or more "Timothies" of our own on a consistent basis. There are also those relationships that one of my daughters nicknamed "The Barnabi." These are the people that we walk through life with shoulder to shoulder — the "iron sharpens iron" relationships (Proverbs 27:17). In my own life right now, I have nine "Timothies" and a number of "Barnabi", including my wife, Kathryn. The point is this: if we are really going to represent Jesus and his mission well, then these relationships have to be happening to equip, to empower, to encourage, and even to admonish us when necessary, so that we stay on course with our mission and produce the fruit we are supposed to produce. You will see that key people in the New Testament story all have these kinds of relationships, and we must as well.

So there is that pattern given in 2 Timothy 2:1-2: Paul to Timothy, Timothy to reliable people, reliable people to others, and so on and so on. We should be seeing this pattern still today. What does it look like for us?

First, **be discipled.** We never get too old or too mature, this side of heaven, to stop being discipled. Let me emphasize this. I have both a Masters and Doctorate. I have been in ministry over 35 years. I have led ministries on the local, regional and national level. And I still need the investment of a "Paul" in my life. You do too! We will never actually "arrive" until we are standing before Jesus. We begin by thinking about how this develops within our community. This is not something we can do on our own. It was not designed to work that way. All of the apostles were in "Timothy" and "Barnabas" relationships. I believe, after thirty years of ministry, many of those spent working with churches to get them back on task, that the primary reason Christians in North America are not making disciples as they should is because they are not first in Paul, Timothy and Barnabas relationships themselves. Their reservoirs are not being filled by a Paul relationship, nor are they being sharpened in Barnabas relationships, so they are not pouring into Timothy relationships. We must be discipled!

Disciple "reliable others." Who are the reliable others? Paul teaches Timothy that he should take what he has learned from him and entrust it to others who are *reliable* and *qualified* to teach others. Paul was helping Timothy to understand that what he was receiving was not just for his own benefit. Many

Christians love to be taught — they are adept at receiving instruction and the example of others. But it is not as common to see them turn around and begin investing those lessons into the lives of other people. Truth be told, most Christians in the West want to be taught, not discipled. Teaching is for one's own benefit; discipling is generational.

If we look at the discipling relationships in the New Testament, such as Paul and Timothy or Paul and Titus, there are at least four characteristics of reliable people that we can see. First, reliable others are seekers of real truth. **They are hungry**, not for position in the church, but for Jesus. They process and purge, change and stretch. The more they learn, the hungrier they become for Jesus.

Next, they will be **open and responsive**. Some may wrestle with the process and argue, but those who are open and responsive never have an argumentative spirit. They don't get into dialogs with us to debate and argue for the sake of debate and argument, but because this is the way they process – the way they uncover the truth. They accept the invitation to a relationship filled with challenge. There is an early indication of their willingness to surrender to Christ. The actual surrender may take some time, but you can see they are contemplating and not rejecting it. Think for a moment of the story of Nicodemus and Jesus (John 3). Nicodemus came to Jesus and debated with him, but not because he was a debater. He was genuinely trying to understand. I tell people that I am not interested in an argument, but for people who are wrestling, I have all the time in the world.

Third, reliable others are **willing to count the cost**. They will respond to the challenge you place on their lives. They not only respond to your challenge in their life to grow, but they early begin processing what it will mean for them to be a faithful follower of Christ. They are willing to rearrange their schedule, their lives, and even some of their relationships, if necessary.

Last, they are people who are **willing to continue the pattern** — some right away! Before they are even taught to multiply by discipling others, they are already enthusiastically talking to others about what they are learning. Take a look at Jesus' disciples for example. As soon as Andrew met Jesus, he went to get Peter. As soon as Philip met Jesus, he went and told Nathaniel. As soon as Matthew was called away from his tax collector table, he threw a huge party for all his "tax collector and sinner" friends, so that they could meet Jesus. And the woman at the well — well, she invited the whole town to come back with her to meet the man who told her everything she had ever done!

Who these people are should be discerned primarily by prayer. Jesus is our example on that. He spent all night praying before he selected his disciples. "[12] *One of those days Jesus went out to a mountainside to pray, and spent the night praying to God.* [13] *When morning came, he called his disciples to him and chose twelve of them, whom he also designated apostles."* (Luke 6:12-13). We have some barometers to measure whether they are reliable, but it is not truly possible to know that they are reliable until we engage them. If they are not reliable, they will self-select out. Be prepared, some people will walk with you for a while, but when they count the cost, they will walk away. It's always disappointing, but sometimes people we thought were *reliable* turn out to be fickle, erratic or even unfaithful. They will decide this "discipleship thing" is really not for them. They were never really "all in" to begin with. Letting them go is often hard, but that's how we can continue to ensure our investment is in *reliable* people, as it must be.

Disciples make disciples. Disciples are not mature and obedient until they are multiplying themselves. The Bible-believing American church is filled with *believers* who are clearly *not* mature disciples because they are not regularly reproducing disciples. Disciple making in this way is not something we add to our schedules, it is the way we live — as we go through life. It's not a burden. It is part of our lifestyle. As we go through every part of our life, we make disciples.

When we disciple this way, there are several outcomes that can be seen in 2 Timothy 2:3-7. Disciples who follow this pattern develop all of the following abilities.

They are able to endure hardship for the kingdom. *"Join with me in suffering, like a good soldier of Christ Jesus."* (v. 3) As a reliable person is disciplined toward maturity in Christ, they become better prepared to handle tough circumstances. They are equipped for life's challenges and sacrifices. They are equipped to handle the opposition to the kingdom rule and reign of Jesus that essentially comes from three sources: the devil, the unsaved world around us and our own flesh (sinful nature). They are better equipped to handle the opposition they will daily face from within themselves and from the forces of this dark world.

They are able to stay on the kingdom task. *"No one serving as a soldier gets entangled in civilian affairs,"* (v. 4a) The last thing Satan wants is an additional *reliable* disciple! If he cannot dissuade us by challenge and hardship, he will. He works hard to distract us with other things. Reliable people grow in their kingdom focus as they are discipled. They stay on the kingdom task, both as it relates to their own growth as a follower of Christ, and also as it relates to their kingdom investment in others. We are able, when we are in these discipling relationships, to remain focused and not become distracted. This promise of focus is a comfort for those of us, like me, who are always in "squirrel mode." For those who may not be familiar with "squirrel mode," the character Doug the Dog from the movie *Up,* was constantly being distracted by every squirrel that went running by.[11] We are not distracted from our own personal growth as a follower of Jesus and our own investment in other people. Here is a personal example — I was greatly encouraged a short time ago by someone that I am discipling. This person is, by his own admission, a rather challenging individual. The past keeps getting in his way. This person made the statement on Facebook that there was no way I could understand how much he appreciated our one-on-one time together. That helped me understand just

---

11   *Up.* Directed by Pete Docter. Pixar, 2009.

how much difference our discipling time is making for him. Sometimes when you feel like you are not getting traction, you realize the person you are discipling is indeed staying on task.

They are able to please King Jesus, our "commanding officer." *"...but rather tries to please his commanding officer."* (v. 4b) — We can know that we are living in a way that pleases Jesus. We can know that we are demonstrating how much we love him. We can grow to a place where we are consistently obeying his commands and living by his example — not because we have rules we *must* follow — but because our heart is being transformed and we *want* to be faithful.

They are able to obey the rules. *"Similarly, anyone who competes as an athlete does not receive the victor's crown except by competing according to the rules."* (v. 5) This is kingdom obedience — not blind servitude. The deeper we grow as a disciple of Jesus, the more we are inwardly transformed. We transition from surrendering to commands externally imposed upon us to being led by a changed heart that desires what Jesus desires. We lovingly live lives of kingdom obedience that naturally live out the culture of Christ's kingdom rule and reign. Our living exemplifies the Beatitudes, which are the descriptors of the rules and culture of the *real* kingdom. We show, by our example that Jesus' teachings are not just some nice teachings of some wise person over two thousand years ago, but they are real and fruit-bearing today.

They are able to enjoy the victory. *"Similarly, anyone who competes as an athlete does not receive the victor's crown except by competing according to the rules."* (v. 5) How many of us want to live from victory to victory? (1 Cor. 15:57) We can enjoy the victory. Even though the life of a disciple may be filled with challenges, reliable disciples experience authentic victory in Christ. They experience *freedom* — overcoming sin and self-centeredness. They are also able to see and rejoice over the kingdom accomplishments they see around them, and especially those wrought by the Lord through their own life and witness. This brings us to the next outcome.

They are able to produce fruit. *"The hardworking farmer should be the first to receive a share of the crops."* (v. 6) In verse six, the focus is on the one who farms. Paul is explaining to Timothy that it is the farmer who is able to first enjoy the fruits of his farming. It is more blessed to give than to receive. This fruit-bearing is not self-seeking, but Jesus does bless you for doing this work. Jesus does help you to enjoy what you are producing. Just as the farmer is the first to enjoy the crops from his own fields, you get to enjoy the growth you see in your disciples. We become more like Jesus in this process of expanding his kingdom. I can tell you this. The main reason I have remained a pastor all these years is the joy of seeing my congregants grow as disciples of Christ and produce fruit. There is no drug anyone could possibly take that would be more addicting than seeing the fruit of your own labor working faithfully alongside Jesus Christ!

They are able to have the Lord's insight in these things. *"Reflect on what I am saying, for the Lord will give you insight into all this."* (v. 7) Finally, Paul tells us in verse seven, that we can have Jesus' own insight. Disciples do not just grow in their endurance, faithfulness and fruitfulness, they also grow in depth of godly insight. They grow in wisdom. They enjoy a deeper understanding of Jesus and the world around them through his eyes. We enjoy deeper understanding of Jesus, what he has done, our relationship with him, and also what he is doing in the world around us.

I have talked about some of the characteristics of the Western church — the church that has largely lost its mission. One of these characteristics is a passionate pursuit of politics. One reason I believe the American church has become so invested in politics is because they've divorced themselves from their real mission of disciple making. As a consequence, the only hope they have for change in the world around them is through legislation and government, and that is sad. It is time for us to get back to Jesus' original mission for us: making disciples.

Into whom are you investing?

Lord, as we talk about disciples becoming disciple-makers, my prayer today is that you would begin convicting all of us about these relationships. It is so easy to just live life on autopilot. And I confess that I am guilty of this myself. Help us to pay attention to the relational aspect that you have embedded in your kingdom — in disciple making. It is so easy to be distracted by the work that we miss the point. And so my prayer is that today you would stop us in our tracks and convict us of that distraction. Compel us to go back and look at the pattern you have given us. Open our minds. Open our eyes. Open our ears, Lord, to hear what the Spirit is saying to us, and then help us to be faithful to walk it out, so that we can be the church you designed and called us to be. Be our teacher. Amen.

Questions for Reflection and Application:

1. Review the graphic at the beginning of the chapter. How do you fit into this sequence? Who are the "Pauls," "Timothies," and the "Barnabases" in your life right now? If one or more of these are missing, what can you do to begin developing these relationships?

2. Look back at the section, "Disciple Reliable Others." Who in your life right now is showing signs of spiritual reliability? Are you currently in a disciple making relationship with them? Should you be? How might you invite them into such a relationship?

3. Consider the questions below, based on characteristics of mature disciples following the pattern of 2 Timothy 2:3-7.

   - Who has God used to help you grow in each of these areas? How are you investing in others to help them experience similar growth?

   - How have you grown in your abilities to endure hardship for Jesus' kingdom?

   - Is your resolve to stay on kingdom task increasing?

   - How have you grown in your ability to faithfully please Jesus?

   - Is your loving obedience increasing or improving?

- Is your freedom in Christ expanding?

- How has your kingdom fruitfulness increased?

- How has your spiritual insight and wisdom grown?

CHAPTER SIX
Disciples Are "All In"

A certain ruler asked him, "Good teacher, what must I do to inherit eternal life?"

"Why do you call me good?" Jesus answered. "No one is good—except God alone. You know the commandments: 'Do not commit adultery, do not murder, do not steal, do not give false testimony, honor your father and mother.'"

"All these I have kept since I was a boy," he said.

When Jesus heard this, he said to him, "You still lack one thing. Sell everything you have and give to the poor, and you will have treasure in heaven. Then come, follow me."

When he heard this, he became very sad, because he was a man of great wealth. Jesus looked at him and said, "How hard it is for the rich to enter the kingdom of God! Indeed, it is easier for a camel to go through the eye of a needle than for a rich man to enter the kingdom of God."

Those who heard this asked, "Who then can be saved?"

Jesus replied, "What is impossible with men is possible with God."

Peter said to him, "We have left all we had to follow you!"

> *"I tell you the truth,"* Jesus said to them, *"no one who has left home or wife or brothers or parents or children for the sake of the kingdom of God will fail to receive many times as much in this age and, in the age to come, eternal life."* (Luke 18:18-30 NIV)

Jesus' disciples down through the ages are devoted to him, devoted to his people (the Church), and devoted to his mission. They are "all in." The problem everyone faces is that we are entangled in the stuff of this fallen world. This is especially true among Christians in the more affluent nations of the world. We have to release our grip on such things in order to truly comprehend the magnitude of our Savior's glorious kingdom.

Jesus sits on the throne of heaven, looking at us wallowing in all that we treasure and pursue, and he calls us to something incredibly better. He calls us to freedom from what binds us. He sees our human "treasure" for what it really is.

Have you ever watched The Learning Channel's documentary show, *Hoarding: Buried Alive?* It can be very disturbing. One morning, while praying about the need to release my heart from my earthly treasure, the Lord reminded me of the single episode I watched over a decade ago (about a woman named

Denise)[12]. Over the next few minutes in prayer, the Lord showed me the "value" of most of what I treasure. I think many of us as affluent Christians fail to realize just how much bondage we have to our stuff – and the stuff that surrounds us is really not that eternally important.

I'm not advocating that we just give everything away; however, I am reflecting even as I write this paragraph about how we are often more devoted to our stuff than we are to Jesus and his mission. In Luke 18, Jesus is teaching and people begin bringing their babies to him so that he can touch (and presumably bless) them. The disciples become frustrated with these people and rebuke the parents. Jesus corrects them there and then. *"Let the little children come to me, and do not hinder them, for the kingdom of God belongs to such as these. I tell you the truth, anyone who will not receive the kingdom of God like a little child will never enter it."* (Luke 18:15-17 NIV)

Children receive very differently than most adults. They receive with trust and enthusiasm. Adults have learned to be more cynical from personal experience in this world. And once we do receive, then we tend to protect what we've got. We lock our cars. We lock our homes. We lock our suitcases on a trip. We lock our phones. We install alarms. We install security cameras. We join neighborhood watch programs.

---

12   www.tlc.com. You can watch the preview of that episode at https://www.youtube.com/watch?v=NY16aLaF_ZE

Somewhere in the audience is one we have come to call "The Rich Young Ruler." He has likely just witnessed Jesus' rebuke over the kids. And it is in Jesus' encounter with this young man that we learn some really important principles about living a fully surrendered, "all in" life.

Jesus knows us – our uniqueness. The young man poses a question to Jesus, *"Good teacher, what must I do to inherit eternal life?"* (Luke 18:18) I have often wondered if he didn't immediately regret asking the question. Jesus takes the interaction in a direction I'm sure the young ruler did not anticipate.

Jesus begins with God. Only God is truly good. The young man was probably just showing respect in calling Jesus "Good Teacher," but Jesus uses his greeting to make a point. Only God is good. The rest of us are flawed by sin. After humanity chose the sinful path following the Creation (Genesis 3), everything about us has been tainted by that sin. In the words of the Apostle Paul as he quotes several passages from the Old Testament in his letter to the Christians at Rome,

> *"There is no one righteous, not even one; there is no one who understands, no one who seeks God. All have turned away, they have together become worthless; there is no one who does good, not even one."*
> (Romans 3:10-12 NIV)

And what the young ruler is about to learn is that Jesus sees his entire life's focus is flawed because of sin.

Jesus challenges him on his "good works" focus. They talk about keeping the Ten Commandments and the man informs Jesus that he has kept all of them since he was a boy. Jesus knows this is a human impossibility. Faithful as this young man may be, he has not really kept the commandments.

Jesus then changes the subject and calls out the young man's idol. *"You still lack one thing. Sell everything you have and give to the poor, and you will have treasure in heaven. Then come, follow me."* (Luke 18:22) Like so many of us, our affluence – our money, our homes, our stuff – has become more important to us than fully following Jesus. This is idolatry. Whenever something is a favored choice for us over Jesus, we are worshiping a false god.

Jesus successfully exposes the young man's heart. Though he may have truly wanted to follow Jesus, his love of money got in the way. The scripture tells us that he became very sad because he was a man of great wealth. Jesus responds, *"How hard it is for the rich to enter the kingdom of God!"* (Luke 18:24). Jesus is able to get right down to his heart because he knows him inside and out! And he knows each of us in the very same way.

Jesus knows our weakness – what distracts us from the life he has for us. I could be the rich young ruler. What about you? Jesus knows every single human being intimately. He is not just God the Redeemer, but God the Creator. He knows each one of us better than we know ourselves. He made us. He knows our divine design. He knows what makes us flourish, and what breaks our spirit. He knows what sin has done to us – the damage it has inflicted. He knows those areas of our lives where we are stuck. He knows what will cause us to stumble. He knows where we are most likely to fail and fall.

Jesus asks us to surrender to him what holds us in bondage. If we are going to get stuck or derailed in some area of life, it will be because we are holding on to something Jesus bids us to release. My friend and colleague, Steven Barr, Leader of Cast Member Church, a global movement among the Walt Disney Parks and Resorts in Anaheim, Orlando, Paris, Tokyo, Hong Kong, and Shanghai, has written an awesome book about living the adventure for which God created us. It was Steven that helped me to see our "stuckness" in life is because we are trusting in something other than God for our comfort, our credibility or for control[13]. Jesus wants us to find these things in him!

Jesus asks us to surrender to him what is of lesser value. If you and I are going to be "all in," then we need to get a grasp on how incredibly valuable the kingdom of God is! C.S. Lewis gives us a great illustration on this truth:

> It would seem that Our Lord finds our desires not too strong, but too weak. We are half-hearted creatures, fooling about with drink and sex and ambition when infinite joy is offered us, like an ignorant child who wants

---

13   Steven L. Barr. *A Guide to a Life Beyond Imagination: Discover the Clarity, Courage, and Confidence to Live the Adventure You Were Created For.* Auburndale FL: Aletheia Press, 2019, pp. 145-152.

to go on making mud pies in a slum because he cannot imagine what is meant by the offer of a holiday at the sea. We are far too easily pleased.[14]

It is inconceivable to many Christians that a fully surrendered life is truly of more value than all of the tangible treasures they have, that can be held in their very hands. But the truth is that what Christ offers is of infinitely more worth.

Jesus invites us to follow Him. Jesus' love is unconditional. Jesus' offer to be his disciples is not. In fact, it costs us everything. To be an "all in" disciple means we must accept the terms of full surrender to him. It is only after the young man in our passage sells *everything*, blessing the poor, that Jesus says, *"then come, follow me."* (Luke 18:22) The disciple's life is not Jesus plus anything else. Everything we are and everything we have belongs to him. The Apostle Paul writes to the Christians at Corinth, *"You are not your own; you were bought with a price."* (1 Corinthians 6:19-20). While we may not have to literally give it all away, when we bow to Jesus for our salvation, we turn the ownership of everything to him.

When we moved from Minnesota to the Orlando area many years ago, God gave us an incredible deal on an enormous home. It was bigger than we had planned to purchase, but it was being sold quickly because the owner had been unable to finish a significant "flip" of the house and was out of money. We got much more home for our money than we could have imagined.

---
14   C.S. Lewis. *The Weight of Glory*. San Francisco CA: HarperOne, 2001.

We have spent the years living in this home completing the flip and then doing our own significant renovations and remodeling. It has been an adventure. And the home is now worth more than twice what we paid for it. Kathryn and I take great joy in our home, but we are careful not to take pride in it. Because even though the mortgage and title deed have our names on them, we know this house doesn't belong to us. And with that open-hearted perspective, we have been incredibly blessed to use this home for his purposes over and over again. We planted a church in it. We have housed many people over the years, enjoying the opportunities God has given us to disciple and mentor those who have lived with us. We've given everything up to follow Jesus, and in return he has blessed us more than we can imagine.

Jesus knows how hard it is for us to give up everything. Our tenacity to cling to earthly stuff is not a surprise to him. Jesus knows full well the extent of sin's damage on every area of our lives, including greed and selfishness. Jesus teaches the crowd around him, *"How hard it is for the rich to enter the kingdom of God!"* (Luke 18:24). If we understand that kingdom, here, really means the dominion of God and not the domain (the rule and reign of God, not the realm), things become a little clearer. I have a friend who likes to say, "You can't say 'Lord' and 'no' in the same sentence!" To be fully surrendered to Jesus is to fully surrender our will to his will.

Jesus knows the unimaginable value of what we will receive if we make the choice. As Jesus is finishing up his lesson, and the rich young ruler has departed in his grief, Peter pipes up,

"We have left all we have to follow you!" (Luke 18:28) Jesus' response to Peter is both precious and powerful. *"I tell you the truth, no one who has left home or wife or brothers or parents or children for the sake of the kingdom of God will fail to receive many times as much in this age and, in the age to come, eternal life."* (Luke 18:29-30 NIV) It is beyond our imagination to grasp the value of a fully devoted life. We can see the sacrifice it requires, but I don't know that we can truly see its benefits. Paul writes to the Christians in Corinth, *"What no eye has seen, what no ear has heard, and what no human mind has conceived" — the things God has prepared for those who love him..."* (1 Corinthians 2:9). Even when we can't fully understand, it's worth it.

Jesus asks us to choose. Children tend to receive with trust. Adults don't. The rich young ruler walked away sad. Satan and our flesh work overtime to make us question the goodness of our God. Since the debacle in Eden, humanity has repeatedly failed to trust God. Adam and Eve concluded God was holding out on them. Abraham and Sarah didn't trust God's promise for an heir. The Hebrew people didn't trust God in the wilderness. They failed to trust again when the spies came back from the Promised Land. Peter didn't trust Jesus on the night of his betrayal. Ananias and Saphira didn't fully trust God and were over enamored with their property. We struggle in the same way. Jesus takes us back to the goodness of God and then offers us the choice.

Disciples of Jesus are "all in," friend. What will you choose? Will you jump in with both feet and enjoy a full life in Christ? Or will you hold on to your old life and stuff like a hoarder and wallow in a decrepit mess of your own making, thinking it's more secure than what Jesus offers?

The choice is yours.

Questions for Reflection and Application:

1. Being a disciple of Jesus is costly. What "stuff" in your life have you had to relinquish in order to be fully devoted to Jesus? What relationships have you had to change or give up? Is there remaining "stuff" you should give up? If so, what is it?

2. What treasures of this world have gotten in your way as you have pursued real devotion to Jesus, to his people (the Church) and his mission?

3. In what ways can you personally relate to the Rich Young Ruler, unable (or at least struggling) to give away those things that stand in the way of an "all in" relationship with Jesus?

4. As you inventory your own life, how are you using everything for God's purposes? Is there something in your life you are still withholding?

5. In what areas of your life are you still struggling to fully trust Jesus?

NEXT STEPS

Now that you've read the book, spend some time prayerfully considering these questions.

1. How would you define a disciple? Are you one? How well is your church fulling the mandate to make such disciples? How can you help your church grow in obedience to this divine directive?

2. How devoted are you to King Jesus? Are you truly devoted, or are you more committed? How do you put your devotion to King Jesus on display for others to see each day? And how are you intentionally leading others to grow in their devotion to King Jesus?

3. How devoted are you to Jesus' people (the Church)? Are you truly devoted, or do you just enjoy their company and the way they "do church"? How do you put your devotion to Jesus people on display? In what ways do you consistently act out this devotion? And how are you intentionally leading others to grow in their devotion to the Church?

4. How would you define Jesus' mission? How devoted are you to that mission? Are you truly devoted to it or is it more of a commitment to support the mission as other carry it out? What is your unique role in Jesus' mission? And how are you intentionally leading others to grow in their devotion to that mission?

5. How fruitful have you been in making disciples yourself? What do you need to grow in this area? If making disciples is the primary metric by which Jesus will measure your devotion to him when you stand before him in glory, how will you fare?

6. Who are your "Pauls"? Who are your "Timothies"? Who are your "Barnabi"? And who should you invited into these relationships?

7. What steps will you now take to become more fully surrendered to Jesus?